Liquid Fea

Liquid Fear

Zygmunt Bauman

polity

First published in 2006 by Polity Press

Polity Press
65 Bridge Street
Cambridge CB2 1UR, UK

Polity Press
350 Main Street
Malden, MA 02148, USA

ISBN-10: 0-7456-3679-9
ISBN-13: 978-07456-3679-5
ISBN-10: 0-7456-3680-2 (pb)
ISBN-13: 978-07456-3680-1 (pb)

A catalogue record for this book is available from the British Library.

Typeset in 11 on 13 pt Sabon
by SNP Best-set Typesetter Ltd, Hong Kong
Printed and bound in Great Britain by MPG Books Ltd, Bodmin, Cornwall

For further information on Polity, visit our website: www.polity.co.uk

Contents

Introduction:
On the Origin, Dynamics
and Uses of Fear

Fear has many eyes
And can see things underground
                    Miguel de (Saavedra) Cervantes, *Don Quixote*

You don't need a reason to be afraid ... I got frightened, but it is
good to be afraid knowing why ...
                    Émile Ajar (Romain Gary), *La Vie en soi*

Let me assert my firm belief that the only thing we have to fear
is fear itself.
                    Franklin Delano Roosevelt, *Inaugural Address*, 1933

Bizarre, yet quite common and familiar to all of us, is the relief
we feel, and the sudden influx of energy, and courage, when after
a long time of uneasiness, anxiety, dark premonitions, days full
of apprehension and sleepless nights, we finally confront the real
danger: a menace we can see and touch. Or perhaps this experience is not as bizarre as it seems if, at long last, we come to know
what was standing behind that vague but obstinate feeling of
something awful and bound to happen which kept poisoning the
days we should be enjoying, yet somehow could not – and which
made our nights sleepless ... Now that we know where the blow
is coming from, we know also what, if anything, we can do to
repel it – or at least we've learned just how limited our ability is
to emerge unharmed and what kind of loss, or injury, or pain we
have to accept.

We have all heard stories about cowards who turned into fearless fighters when they were faced with a 'real danger'; when the disaster they had been expecting day in, day out, but had tried in vain to imagine, finally struck. Fear is at its most fearsome when it is diffuse, scattered, unclear, unattached, unanchored, free floating, with no clear address or cause; when it haunts us with no visible rhyme or reason, when the menace we should be afraid of can be glimpsed everywhere but is nowhere to be seen. 'Fear' is the name we give to our *uncertainty*: to our *ignorance* of the threat and of what is to be *done* – what can and what can't be – to stop it in its tracks – or to fight it back if stopping it is beyond our power.

The experience of living in sixteenth-century Europe – the time and the place when and where our modern era was about to be born – was crisply, and famously, summed up by Lucien Febvre in just four words: 'Peur toujours, peur partout' ('fear always and everywhere').[1] Febvre connected that ubiquitousness of fear to darkness, which started just on the other side of the hut door and wrapped the world beyond the farm fence; in the darkness anything may happen, but there is no telling what will. Darkness is not the cause of danger, but it is the natural habitat of uncertainty – and so of fear.

Modernity was to be the great leap forward: away from that fear and into a world free of blind and impermeable fate – that greenhouse of fears. As Victor Hugo ruminated,[2] wistfully and waxing lyrical on occasion: ushered in by science ('the political tribune will be transformed into a scientific one'), a time will come of an end to surprises, calamities, catastrophes – but also of an end to disputes, illusions, parasitisms . . . In other worlds, a time free of all that stuff of which fears are made. What was to be a route of escape, however, proved instead to be a long detour. Five centuries later, to us standing at the other end of the huge graveyard of dashed hopes, Febvre's verdict sounds – again – remarkably apt and topical. Ours is, again, a time of fears.

Fear is a feeling known to every living creature. Humans share that experience with the animals. Students of animal behaviour have described in great detail the rich repertoire of animal responses to the immediate presence of a menace threatening their life – which all, as in the case of humans facing a threat, veer between the alternatives of escape and aggression. Humans, however, know in addition something else: a sort of 'second degree' fear, a fear, so to speak, socially and culturally 'recycled', or (as Hugues Lagrange in his fundamental study of fear calls it)[3] a 'derivative fear' that guides their behaviour (having first re-formed their perception of the world and the expectations guiding their behavioural choices) whether or not a menace is immediately present. Secondary fear may be seen as a sediment of a past expe-rience of facing the menace point blank – a sediment that outlives the encounter and becomes an important factor in shaping human conduct even if there is no longer a direct threat to life or integrity.

'Derivative fear' is a steady frame of mind that is best described as the sentiment of being *susceptible* to danger; a feeling of inse-curity (the world is full of dangers that may strike at any time with little or no warning) and vulnerability (in the event of the danger striking, there will be little if any chance of escape or suc-cessful defence; the assumption of vulnerability to dangers depends more on a lack of trust in the defences available than on the volume or nature of actual threats). A person who has interiorized such a vision of the world that includes insecurity and vulnerabil-ity will routinely, even in the absence of a genuine threat, resort to the responses proper to a point-blank meeting with danger; 'derivative fear' acquires a self-propelling capacity.

It has been, for instance, widely noted that the opinion that the 'world out there' is dangerous and better to be avoided is more common among people who seldom, if ever, go out in the eve-nings, when the dangers seem to them most terrifying; and there is no way of knowing whether such people avoid leaving their homes because of their sense of danger, or whether they are afraid of the unspoken dangers lurking in dark streets because, in the absence of practice, they have lost the confidence-giving ability to cope with the presence of a threat, or because, lacking direct personal experiences of threat, they are prone to let their imagina-tions, already afflicted by fear, run loose.

Dangers one is afraid of (and so also the derivative fears they arouse) may be of three kinds. Some threaten the body and the possessions. Some others are of a more general nature, threatening the durability and reliability of the social order on which security of livelihood (income, employment), or survival in the case of invalidity or old age, depend. Then there are dangers that threaten one's place in the world – a position in the social hierarchy, identity (class, gender, ethnic, religious), and more generally an immunity to social degradation and exclusion. Numerous studies show, however, that 'derivative fear' is easily 'decoupled' in the sufferers' awareness from the dangers that cause it. People it afflicts with the sentiment of insecurity and vulnerability may interpret a derivative fear by reference to any of the three types of dangers – independently of (and often in defiance of) the evidence of their relative contributions and responsibility. The resulting defensive or aggressive reactions aimed at mitigating the fear may be therefore targeted away from the dangers truly responsible for the presumption of insecurity.

For instance, the state, having founded its *raison d'être* and its claim to citizens' obedience on the promise to protect its subjects against threats to their existence, but no longer able to deliver on its promise (particularly the promise of defence against the second and third types of danger) – or able responsibly to reaffirm it in view of the fast globalizing and increasingly extraterritorial markets – is obliged to shift the emphasis of 'fear protection' from dangers to social security to the dangers to personal safety. It then 'subsidiarizes' the battle against fears 'down' to the realm of individually run and managed 'life politics', while simultaneously contracting out the supply of battle weapons to the consumer markets.

Most fearsome is the ubiquity of fears; they may leak out of any nook or cranny of our homes and our planet. From dark streets and from brightly lit television screens. From our bedrooms and our kitchens. From our workplaces and from the underground train we take to get there or back. From people we meet and people whom we failed to notice. From something we ingested and something with which our bodies came in touch. From what we call 'nature' (prone, as hardly ever before in our memory, to devastate our homes and workplaces and threatening to destroy our bodies through the proliferation of earthquakes, floods, hurricanes, mudslides, droughts or heat waves), or from other people (prone, as hardly ever before in our memory, to devastate our homes and workplaces and threatening to destroy our bodies through the sudden abundance of terrorist atrocities, violent crime, sexual assaults, poisonous food and polluted air or water).

There is also that third, perhaps the most terrifying, zone, a sense-numbing and mind-chafing grey zone, as yet unnamed, from which ever more dense and sinister fears seep, threatening to destroy our homes, workplaces and bodies through disasters – natural but not quite, human but not completely, natural and human at the same time though unlike either of them. The zone of which some over-ambitious yet hapless accident-and-calamity-prone sorcerer's apprentice, or a malicious genie imprudently let out of the bottle, must have taken charge. The zone where power grids go bust, petrol taps run dry, stock exchanges collapse, all-powerful companies disappear together with dozens of services one used to take for granted and thousands of jobs one used to believe to be rock-solid, where jets crash together with their thousand-and-one safety gadgets and hundreds of passengers, market caprices make worthless the most precious and coveted of assets, and any other imaginable or unimaginable catastrophes brew (or perhaps are brewed?) ready to overwhelm the prudent and the imprudent alike. Day in, day out we learn that the inventory of dangers is far from complete: new dangers are discovered and announced almost daily, and there is no knowing how many more of them and of what kind have managed to escape our (and the experts'!) attention – getting ready to strike without warning.

As Craig Brown notes, however, in his chronicle of the 1990s with that inimitable wit which is his trademark:

> everywhere, there was a rise in Global Warning. Every day, there were new Global Warnings about killer viruses, killer waves, killer drugs, killer icebergs, killer meat, killer vaccines, killer killers and other possible causes of imminent death. At first, these Global Warnings were frightening, but after a while people began to enjoy them.[4]

Indeed. Knowing that this is a fearsome world to live in does not mean living in fear – at least not twenty-four hours a day and seven days a week. We have more than enough shrewd stratagems which (if supported with all sorts of clever gadgets obligingly offered by the shops) can help us to avoid such a gruesome eventuality. We can even come to *enjoy* the 'global warnings'. After all, living in a liquid modern world known to admit only one certainty – the certainty that tomorrow can't be, shouldn't be, won't be like it is today – means a daily rehearsal of disappearance, vanishing, effacement and dying; and so, obliquely, a rehearsal of the non-finality of death, of recurrent resurrections and perpetual reincarnations . . .

Like all other forms of human cohabitation, our liquid modern society is a contraption attempting to make life with fear liveable. In other words, a contraption meant to repress the potentially disarming and incapacitating dread of danger, to silence such fears as derive from dangers that can't be, or should not be for the sake of the preservation of social order, effectively prevented. As in the case of many other harrowing and potentially order-disrupting sentiments, this necessary job is done, as Thomas Mathiesen put it, through 'silent silencing' – in a process 'that is quiet rather than noisy, hidden rather than open, unnoticed rather than noticeable, unseen rather than seen, non-physical rather than physical'. 'Silent silencing'

> is structural; it is a part of our everyday life; it is unbounded and is therefore engraved upon us; it is noiseless and therefore passes by unnoticed; and it is dynamic in the sense that in our society it spreads and becomes continually more encompassing. The structural character of the silencing 'exempts' representatives of the state from responsibility for it, its everyday character makes it 'inescapable' from the point of view of those being silenced, its unbounded character makes it especially effective in relation to the individual, its noiseless character makes its easier to legitimise, and its dynamic character turns it into a mechanism of silencing which may be increasingly trusted.[5]

To start with, like everything else in liquid modern life, death is made temporary and until further notice. It lasts until another comeback of a long unremembered celebrity or long uncelebrated tune, until a round-figure anniversary excavation of another long-forgotten writer or painter, or until the arrival of another retro fashion. As bites become common, stings no longer are or feel mortal. This or that disappearance, if it occurs, will hopefully be as revocable as so many others before it have proved to be.

Moreover, many more blows keep being announced as imminent than there are blows that eventually strike, so you can always hope that this or that blow so recently announced will pass you by. Whose computer has been incapacitated by the sinister 'millennium bug'? How many people did you meet who fell victim to the carpet mites? How many of your friends died of mad-cow disease? How many of the people you know have been made ill or invalid by genetically engineered food? Which of your neighbours and acquaintances has been assaulted and maimed by the treacherous and sinister asylum-seekers? Panics come and go, and however frightful they are, you may safely presume that they will share the fate of all the others.

Liquid life flows or plods from one challenge to another and from one episode to another, and the familiar habit of challenges and episodes is that they tend to be short-lived. You may assume as much of the life expectation of the fears currently gripping expectations. What is more, so many fears enter your life complete with the remedies of which you often hear before you have had time to be frightened by the ills which these remedies promise to remedy. The danger of the millennium bug was not the only horrifying news brought to you by the self-same companies which had already offered to make your computer, at a proper price, immune. Catherine Bennett, for instance, laid bare the plot behind the package deal in the case of a 'starter hit' for an expensive therapy which warns that 'the wrong foods are responsible for rapid, premature aging; a tired, drawn and doughy complexion . . . wrinkled, leathery, dried-out looking facial skin . . .' – only to reassure its prospective clients that 'being wrinkle-free for life is achievable if you follow the 28-day programme' – at the cost of a mere 119 pounds sterling.[6]

What the millennium bug affair demonstrated and what Bennett discovered in the case of one miracle fear-defying cosmetic device may be seen as a pattern for infinite numbers of others. The consumer economy depends on the production of consumers, and the consumers that need to be produced for fear-fighting products are fearful and frightened consumers, hopeful that the dangers they fear can be forced to retreat and that they can do it (with paid help, for sure).

This life of ours has proved to be different from the kind of life which the sages of the Enlightenment and their heirs and disciples

envisaged and set out to design. In the new life which they adumbrated and resolved to create, it was hoped that the feat of taming
fears and bridling the menaces that caused them would be a one-
off affair. In the liquid modern setting, however, the struggle
against fears has turned out to be a lifelong task, while fear-
triggering dangers, even when none of them is suspected to be
intractable, have come to be believed to be permanent, *undetach-
able* companions of human life. Our life is anything but fear-free,
and the liquid modern setting in which it is bound to be conducted
is anything but free of dangers and threats. A *whole life* is now a
long and probably unwinnable struggle against the potentially
incapacitating impact of fears, and against the genuine or putative
dangers that make us fearful. It is best seen as a continuous search
for, and perpetual testing of, stratagems and expedients allowing
us to stave off, even if temporarily, the imminence of dangers – or
better yet to shift the worry about them onto a side burner where
they might, hopefully, fizzle out or stay forgotten for the duration.
Our inventiveness knows no bounds. The stratagems are plentiful;
the more profuse they are the more ineffective and the more
inconclusive their effects. Though, with all the differences that set
them apart, they have one precept in common: cheat time and
beat it at its own game. Delay *frustration*, not *gratification*.

The future is foggy? One more sound reason not to let it haunt
you. Dangers unknowable? One more sound reason to put them
aside. So far, so good; it could be worse. Keep it like this. Don't
start worrying about crossing that bridge before you come to it.
Perhaps you'll never come near it, or the bridge will fall to pieces
or move elsewhere before you do. So – why worry now?! Better
to follow the age-old recipe: *carpe diem*. To put it simply: enjoy
now, pay later. Or, prompted by a newer version of that ancient
wisdom, updated courtesy of credit card companies: take the
waiting out of wanting.

We live on credit: no past generation was as heavily in debt as
we are – individually and collectively (the task of state budgets
used to be to balance the books; nowadays, 'good budgets' are
those that keep the excess of spending over income at the last year's
level). Living on credit has its utilitarian pleasures: why delay the
gratification? Why wait, if you can relish future bliss here and
now? Admittedly, the future is beyond control. But the credit card,
magically, brings that vexingly elusive future straight into your lap.

You may consume the future, so to speak, in advance – while there is still something left to be consumed . . . This seems to be the latent attraction of living-on-credit, whose manifest benefit, if you believe the commercials, is purely utilitarian: giving pleasure. And if the future is designed to be as nasty as you suspect it may be, you can consume it now, still fresh and unspoiled, before the disaster strikes and before that future has the chance to show you just how nasty that disaster might be. (This is, to think of it, what the cannibals of yore did, finding in eating their enemies up the surest way of putting paid to the threats those enemies carried: a consumed, digested and excreted enemy was no longer frightening. Though, alas, all the enemies can't be eaten. As more of them are devoured, their ranks seem to swell instead of shrinking.)

Media are messages. Credit cards are also messages. If savings books imply certainty of the future, an uncertain future cries out for credit cards.

Savings books grow out of, and feed on, a future one can trust – a future certain to arrive and, once it has arrived, to be not so dissimilar from the present. A future expected to value what we value – and so to respect past savings and reward their holders. Savings books thrive as well on the hope/expectation/confidence that – thanks to the *continuity* between now and 'then' – what is being done right now, in the present, will pre-empt the 'then', tying up the future before it arrives; what we do *now* will 'make the difference', *determine* the shape of the future.

Credit cards and the debts which credit cards make easy would frighten off the meek and disturb even the adventurous among us. If they don't, it is thanks to our suspicion of *discontinuity*: our premonition that the future that will arrive (*if* it arrives, and if I will still be there to witness its arrival) will be different from the present we know – though there is no knowing in what respect it will differ and how far. Will it, years from now, honour the sacrifices done presently in its name? Will it reward the efforts invested in securing its benevolence? Or perhaps it will on the contrary make today's assets into tomorrow's liabilities and precious loads into vexing burdens? That we don't know and can't know, and there is little point in striving to bind the unknowable.

Some bridges which we tarry in starting to worry about, but which will eventually need to be crossed, are not, however, far enough away for the worry about crossing them to be light-heartedly postponed . . . Not all dangers seem remote enough to be dismissed as no more than fanciful figments of a feverish imagination, or at any rate irrelevant to what has been placed next on our agenda. Fortunately, however, we also have a way to bypass those hurdles that have come too close for comfort and can no longer be neglected: we can think of them, and we do, as 'risks'.

We then admit that the next step to take is 'risky' (may prove to be unacceptably costly, bring closer old dangers or provoke new ones), as all steps tend to be. There is a possibility that we won't get what we want and get instead something quite different and utterly unpleasant, something which we would rather avoid (we call such unpalatable and undesirable consequences 'side-effects', or 'collateral damage', since they are not intended and are located away from the target of our action). We also admit that they can come 'unanticipated', and that notwithstanding all our calculations they may take us by surprise and catch us unprepared. All that having been thought of, pondered and said, we proceed nevertheless (for lack of a better choice) *as if* we *could* anticipate which undesirable consequences require our attention and vigilance and then monitor our steps accordingly. No wonder: it is only about the consequences which we *can* predict that we can worry, and it is only those same consequences that we can struggle to escape. And so it is only the undesirable consequences of such a 'pre-visible' kind that we file in the category of 'risks'. Risks are the dangers whose probability we *can* (or believe that we can) calculate: risks are the *calculable* dangers. Once so defined, risks are the next best thing to (alas unattainable) certainty.

Let's note however that 'calculability' does not mean predictability; what is being calculated is only the *probability* that things go wrong and disaster strikes. Calculations of probability say something reliable about the spread of effects of a large number of similar actions, but are almost worthless as a means of prediction when they are (rather illegitimately) used as a guide for one specific undertaking. Probability, even most earnestly calculated, offers no certainty that the dangers will or will not be avoided in *this* particular case here and now or *that* case there and then. But at least the very fact that we have done our computation of probabilities (and so, by implication, have avoided rash decisions and the charge of recklessness) can give us the courage to decide whether the game is or is not worth the candle, and offer a measure of reassurance, however unwarranted. Getting the probabilities right, we have done something reasonable and perhaps even helpful; now we 'have reason' to consider the probability of bad luck too high to justify the risky measure, or too low to stop us taking our chances.

More often than not, however, switching attention from dangers to risks proves to be another subterfuge; an attempt to evade the problem rather than a passport for safe conduct. As Milan Kundera pointed out in his *Les Testaments trahis*,[7] the setting of our lives is wrapped in fog, not in total darkness, in which we would see nothing and be unable to move: 'in the fog one is free, but this is a freedom of someone in the fog', we can see a thirty or fifty yards ahead, we can admire the beautiful trees alongside the road we walk, note the passers-by and react to their gambits, avoid bumping into others and bypass the boulder or a hole in front – but we can hardly see the crossing further ahead or the car still a few hundred yards away but coming at high speed in our direction. We may say that true to such 'living in fog' our 'certainty' targets and focuses our precautional efforts on the visible, known and near dangers, dangers that *can* be anticipated and *can* have their probability computed – whereas by far the most awesome and fearsome dangers are precisely those that are *impossible*, or excruciatingly *difficult*, to anticipate: the *un*predicted, and in all likelihood *unpredictable* ones.

Busy calculating the risks, we tend to sideline that greater worry and so manage to keep such catastrophes as we are impotent to prevent away from sapping our self-confidence. Focusing on things we can do something about, we are left with no time to occupy ourselves with reflecting on things about which we can't do anything anyway. This helps us to defend our sanity. This keeps nightmares, and insomnia, at a distance. This does not necessarily make us more secure, though.

Nor does it make the dangers less realistic. Our guess/intuition/ suspicion/premonition/conviction/certainty that this is so may take a nap, but it can't be put to sleep forever. Time and again, and recently on a visibly accelerating rate, dangers keep reminding us just how realistic they remain in spite of all the precautionary measures we have taken. On intermittent but quite regular occasions they are excavated from their shallow grave where they have been buried just a few inches below the surface of our awareness, and are brutally cast into the limelight of our attention; obligingly, successive catastrophes proffer such occasions – in profusion.

Several years ago, and a few years before the events of 9/11 the tsunami, Hurricane Katrina and the terrifying leap in petrol prices that followed them (even if mercifully short-lived this time round) supplied such shocking occasions to wake up and sober up, Jacques Attali pondered the phenomenal financial triumph of the film *Titanic*, which outstripped all previous box-office records of apparently similar disaster movies. He offered then the following explanation, strikingly credible when it was written down, but a few years later sounding not short of prophetic:

> *Titanic* is us, our triumphalist, self-congratulating, blind, hypo-critical society, merciless towards its poor – a society in which everything is predicted except the means of predicting . . . (W)e all guess that there is an iceberg waiting for us, hidden somewhere in the misty future, which we will hit and then go down to the sounds of music . . .[8]

Sweet music as it were, soothing yet exhilarating. Live music, real-time music. Latest hits, top celebrity performers. Reverberating sounds that deafen, blinking stroboscopic lights that blind. Making the faint whispers of forebodings inaudible, and the enormity of majestically silent icebergs invisible.

Yes, *icebergs* – not one iceberg, but many, probably too many to count them all. Attali named several: financial, nuclear, ecological, social (unpacking the latter as the prospect of 3 billion 'redundancies' in the planet's population). Were he writing now, in 2005, he would surely lengthen the list – reserving pride of place for either the 'terrorist iceberg' or the 'religious fundamentalism iceberg'. Or, and perhaps most probably, the 'implosion of civilization' iceberg – one that could be recently watched, in the aftermath of Middle Eastern military adventures or Katrina's visit to New Orleans, in a sort of dress rehearsal, and in all its ugly, gruesome monstrosity.

*Im*plosion, not *ex*plosion, so different in shape from the one in which the fears of the 'collapse of the civilized order' – fears that had accompanied our ancestors at least from the time that Hobbes proclaimed *bellum omnium contra omnes*, war of all against all, to be the 'natural state' of humanity – tended to be articulated during the 'solid' phase of the modern era.

There were no revolutionaries in Louisiana and no street battles or barricades on the streets of New Orleans; no one rebelled against the order of things and most certainly no clandestine networks have been discovered plotting assault on the current assortment of laws and the currently binding scheme of order. Calling what happened in and around New Orleans a 'collapse of law and order' cannot grasp the event, let alone its message, fully. Law and order simply vanished – as if they had never existed. Suddenly, learned habits and routines that guided 90 per cent or more of the pursuits of daily life lost their sense – a sense normally too self-evident to grant it a second thought. Tacit assumptions lost their grip. Customary cause-and-effect sequences fell apart. What we call 'normal' on working days or 'civilization' on festive occasions has proved to be, literally, paper-thin. Flood waters soaked, pulped and washed away that paper in no time.

> At Rapides Parish Detention Centre 3 in Alexandria, which normally holds convicted felons, there are now 200 new inmates . . . evacuated from flooded jails in New Orleans.
>
> They have no paperwork indicating whether they are charged with having too much to drink or attempted murder. There is no judge to hear the cases, no courthouse designated to hear them in and no lawyer to represent them . . .
>
> It is an implosion of the legal network not seen since disasters like the Chicago fire in 1871 or the San Francisco earthquake of 1906, events in times so much simpler as to be useless in making much sense of this one.[9]

'No one has any idea who these people are or why they're here' – this is how one of the lawyers delegated to the detention centre summed up the situation. This short sharp statement conveyed more than just the implosion of the formal 'legal network'. And it was not just the detainees, caught up in the middle of a legal procedure, who lost their social denomination, and indeed the identities by which they used to be recognized and which once used to set in motion the chain of acts reflecting/determining their place in the order of things. Many other survivors met the same fate. And not just the survivors . . .

> In the downtown business district here, on a dry stretch of Union Street . . . a corpse . . . Hours passed, the dusk of curfew crept, the body remained . . . Night came, then this morning, then noon, and another sun beat down on a dead son of the Crescent City . . . What is remarkable is that on a downtown street in a major American city, a corpse can decompose for days, like carrion, and that is acceptable. Welcome to New Orleans in the post-apocalypse . . . Scraggly residents emerge from waterlogged wood to say strange things, and then return into the rot. Cars drive the wrong way on the Interstate and no one cares. Fires burn, dogs scavenge, and old signs from les bons temps have been replaced with hand-scrawled threats that looters will be shot dead.

The incomprehensible has become routine.[10]

While the law together with the lawyers vanished from view and the corpses waited in vain for burial, the 'enjoy now, pay later' strategy that made 'civilization as we've come to know it' so gratifying came home to roost. The outburst of compassion and the frantic PR performances of the politicians mitigated the impact for a time and offered a temporary relief to the people burdened with old debts but now deprived of the income which, they had hoped, would have allowed them to repay them; but all that proved to be but a short-lived respite. 'Six to nine months from now,' a *New York Times* reporter predicted, 'FEMA [the federal help agency] will be gone, the church groups will be gone and creditors will once more be demanding their money';[11] 'someone who had a great job just before Katrina may have a very different income today', while 'thousands and thousands of people no longer have checkbooks, insurance papers, car titles (or cars), birth certificates, Social Security cards or wallets' . . . As I write these words, six months have not yet passed, but in the city which used to be one of the jewels in the US crown 'lights are twinkling in dozens of neighbourhoods, but darkness spreads across 40 percent of the city', 'almost half of New Orleans lacks natural gas for cooking or heating', 'toilets in roughly half the homes are still not connected to the city's sewer system' and about a quarter of the city is still without drinkable water.[12] And there is little hope left that things will turn for the better.

> Less than three months after Hurricane Katrina ravaged New Orleans, relief legislation remains dormant in Washington and

despair is growing among officials here who fear that Congress
and the Bush administration are losing interest in their plight . . . the
sense of urgency that spurred action in September is swiftly drain-
ing away.[13]

A few years before Katrina landed on the American shore,
Jean-Pierre Dupuy found a name for what was about to happen:
'the irruption of the possible in the impossible'.[14] And he warned:
to prevent a catastrophe, one needs first to *believe in its possibility*. One needs to believe that the impossible *is* possible. That the
possible *always* lurks, restlessly, inside the protective carapace of
impossibility, waiting to irrupt. No danger is so sinister and no
catastrophe strikes so hard as those that are viewed as of negligible probability; thinking of them as improbable or not thinking
of them at all is the excuse for doing nothing to stop them before
they reach the point at which the improbable turns into reality
and it is suddenly too late to mitigate its impact, let alone to stave
off its arrival. And yet this is precisely what we are doing (not
doing, rather) – daily, unthinkingly. 'The present situation shows
us', observes Dupuy, 'that the announcement of a catastrophe does
not make any visible change, either in our manner of conduct, or
in our way of thinking. Even when they have been informed,
people don't believe what they have learned.'[15] He quotes Corinne
Lepage: 'The mind rejects [such an announcement], telling itself
that this is just not possible.'[16] And concludes: the most awesome
obstacle to the prevention of a catastrophe is its incredibility . . .

'Apocalypse Now' (that very expression is a challenge to our
idea of probability) has been staged again. Not in a cinema or in
the theatre of the imagination, but on the downtown streets of a
major American city. 'Not in Baghdad, not in Rwanda, here' – this
is how Dan Barry, reporting from a city where the impossible
revealed the possibility lying inside, hammers home the novelty
of the production.[17] Apocalypse did not happen this time in the
far-away Vietnam rainforest, where the original staging of *Apocalypse Now* was located; and not on the dark shores of the darkest
of continents where Conrad placed the 'heart of darkness' to make
his message legible to his civilized readers – but *here,* in the heart
of the civilized world, in a city acclaimed for its beauty and *joie
de vivre* and still until a few days before a magnet for millions
of tourists circling the globe in search of high-art delights and

high-class entertainment – those most lauded and most coveted gifts of civilization's creative forces.

Katrina let out civilization's most closely guarded secret: that – as Timothy Garton Ash, in an essay under the tell-all title 'It always lies below' vividly put it – 'the crust of civilization we tread is always wafer thin. One tremor, and you've fallen through, scratching and gouging for your life like a wild dog.'

> I can't avoid the feeling that there will be more of this, much more of it, as we go deeper into the 21st century. There are just too many big problems looming which could push humanity back . . . if large parts of the world were tormented by unpredictable storms, flooding and temperature changes, then what happened in New Orleans would seem like a tea party.
>
> In a sense, these too would be man-made hurricanes ['the consequences of the United States continuing to pump out carbon dioxide as if there were no tomorrow']. But there are also more direct threats of humans towards other humans . . . Suppose there's a dirty bomb or even a small nuclear weapon exploded by a terrorist group in a major city. What then?[18]

Rhetorical questions, to be sure. Ash's message is that the threat of '*de*civilization' (a term Ash spotted in one of Jack London's novels) is frightfully real: 'remove the elementary staples of organized, civilized life – food, shelter, drinkable water, minimal personal security – and we go back within hours to a Hobbesian state of nature, a war of all against all.'

One could quarrel with Ash whether there is such a 'state of nature' to which one could go back, or whether the famed 'war of all against all' is rather a condition emerging at the other end of the 'civilizing process', the moment the 'wafer-thin crust' is broken by the shock of a natural or a human-made catastrophe. Whether there is indeed a 'second line of trenches', however waterlogged, slushy, malodorous and otherwise inhospitable to humans, on which humans groomed by and for 'civilized life' may fall back, once their 'secondary-natural' habitat implodes. Or whether one of the integral aspects of the civilizing process is rather an exactly opposite intention: to prevent the 'going back' by making its human objects 'civilization addicted' and so 'civilization dependent', while stripping them of all alternative skills that would enable interhuman cohabitation in the event that the veneer of civilized manners is washed away. This is, though, I admit, only a somewhat minor, since a 'fringe' quibble – crucial perhaps for philosophers of culture, but by and large absent from, and irrelevant to, the topic under discussion; the topic which, I would suggest, could be best described as the 'Titanic complex' or the 'Titanic syndrome'.

The 'Titanic syndrome' is the horror of falling through the 'wafer-thin crust' of civilization into that nothingness stripped of the 'elementary staples of organized, civilized life' ('civilized' precisely because 'organized' – routine, predictable, balancing the signposting with the behavioural repertoire). Falling singly or in company, but in each case being *evicted* from a world where 'elementary staples' go on being supplied and there is a holding power that can be counted on.

The principal (though silent) *actor* in the Titanic story, as we know, was the iceberg. But it wasn't the iceberg, waiting 'out there' in ambush, that was the *horror* that made the story stand out among the multitude of similar horror/disaster stories. That horror was all that mayhem which happened 'in here', in the bowels of the luxurious liner: like, for instance, the lack of any sensible and workable plan to evacuate and save the passengers of a sinking ship, or the acute shortage of lifeboats and lifebelts – something for which the iceberg 'out there', in the pitch of a sub-Arctic night, served only as a catalyst and a litmus paper rolled into one. That 'something' which '*always* lies below' but waits until we jump into the freezing sub-Arctic waters to be faced with it point-blank. Something all the more horrifying for staying concealed most of the time (perhaps *all* the time) and so taking its victims by surprise whenever it crawls out of its lair, always catching them unprepared and inept to respond.

Concealed? Yes, but never further away than at a skin-deep stretch. Civilization is vulnerable; it always stays but one shock away from inferno. As Stephen Graham poignantly spelled it out, we 'become ever more dependent on complex, distantiated systems for the sustenance of life', and so even 'small disruptions and disablement can have enormous, cascading effects on social, economic and environmental life' – particularly in the cities, where most of the life of most of us is lived, the places 'extremely vulnerable to external disruption'. 'More than ever, the collapse of functioning urban infrastructure grids now brings panic and fears

of the breakdown of the functioning urban social order.'[19] Or as
Martin Pawley, quoted by Graham, put it, 'Fear of the dislocation
of urban services on a massive scale' is now 'endemic in the population of all great cities'.[20]

Endemic . . . Part of daily life. No need of a big catastrophe, as
a small accident will do to set in motion a 'massive dislocation'.
Catastrophe may arrive unannounced – there will be no trumpets
warning that the unassailable walls of Jericho are about to crumble.
There are more than enough reasons to be afraid – and so more
than enough reasons to immerse oneself in sounds of music sufficiently loud to stifle the sounds of cracking walls.

Fears emanating from the Titanic syndrome are fears of a breakdown or a catastrophe that may descend *on us all*, hitting blindly
and indiscriminately, randomly and with no rhyme and reason,
and finding *everyone* unprepared and defenceless. There are,
however, other fears no less, if not more, horrifying: fears of being
picked out from the joyous crowd *singly*, or severally at the utmost,
and condemned to suffer *alone* while all the others go on with
their revelries. Fears of a *personal* catastrophe. Fears of becoming
a selected target, earmarked for personal doom. Fears of falling
out of a fast accelerating vehicle, or being thrown overboard,
while the rest of the riders, with their seatbelts securely buckled,
find the journey ever more entertaining. Fears of being left behind.
Fears of *exclusion*.

That such fears are not at all imaginary you can take on the
leading authority of the media that stand – visibly, tangibly – for a
reality you can neither view nor touch without their help. 'Reality
TV' shows, those liquid modern versions of the ancient 'morality
plays', vouch daily for the rugged reality of fears. As suggested by the
name they have assumed, a name unopposed by their viewers and
questioned only by a few particularly priggish pedants, what they
show is real; more importantly, however, it also suggests that 'real' is
what they show. And what they show is that the inevitability of exclusion, and the fight against being excluded, are what that reality boils
down to. The 'reality shows' need not hammer that message home:
most of their viewers already *know* that truth; it is precisely its deep-
seated familiarity that draws them to the screens in droves.

As it happens, we tend to find something pleasingly comforting
in listening to the tunes we know by heart. And we tend to believe

what we *see* much more than we tend to trust what we *hear*. Think of the difference between 'eye-witnessing' and 'mere hearsay' (have you ever heard about 'ear-witness' or 'mere see-say'?). Images are so much more 'real' than printed or spoken words. The stories they tell hide the story-teller, 'he (she) who could lie' and so misinform. Unlike human go-betweens, cameras (or so we have been trained to believe) 'do not lie', they 'tell the truth'. Thanks to the image, each one of us can get, as Edmund Husserl (who more than any other philosopher was consumed by the desire to find the foolproof, error-free way of getting down to the 'truth of the matter') wished to, *zurück zu dem Sachen selbst* – 'back to the things themselves'. When confronted with a photographically/electronically contrived image, nothing seems to stand between us and reality; nothing that may arrest or divert the eye. 'Seeing is believing' means that 'I'll believe it when I see it', but it also means that 'what I'll see, I'll believe'. And what we see is *people trying to exclude other people to avoid being excluded by them.* A banal truth for most of us – though one that we avoid, with a measure of success, articulating. 'Reality TV' did it for us – and we are grateful. The knowledge which 'reality TV' spells out would otherwise be diffuse, sliced into bits and pieces notoriously difficult to collate and make sense of.

What (whether deliberately or inadvertently, explicitly or obliquely) the 'reality TV shows' help us to find out, for instance, is that our political institutions on which we came to rely in case of trouble, and which we have been taught to see as the warrants of our safety, form – as John Dunn recently pointed out – a contraption adjusted to the servicing of the 'order of egoism', and that the main construction principle of that order is the 'wager on the strong' – 'a wager on the rich, to some degree perforce on those with the good fortune to be rich already, but above all on those with the skill, nerve and luck to make themselves so'.[21] But when it comes to evacuating a sinking ship or finding a seat on a lifeboat, skill and nerve prove to be of little help. Perhaps luck is then the only salvation – but luck, notoriously, is a rare gift of fate, one of those gifts that are few and far between.

Millions find that sombre truth daily – as did Jerry Roy of Flint, Michigan, who joined the General Motors company three decades ago but now 'faces the prospect of either losing his job or accepting a sharp pay cut' as 'the GM that was once an unassailable symbol of the nation's industrial might' has become 'a shadow of its former self, and the post-World War II promise of blue-collar factory work being a secure path to the American dream has faded with it'. What help can skills and nerve be when 'all these places that used to be factories are now just parking lots', while the company that owned them 'is moving to rewrite or even tear up its labour contracts', seeking 'major cuts in the health care and pension benefits', and shifting 'thousands of jobs overseas'?[22]

Occasions to be afraid are one of the few things of which our times, badly missing certainty, security and safety, are not short. Fears are many and varied. People of different social, gender and age categories are haunted by their own; there are also fears that we all share – in whatever part of the globe we happen to have been born or have chosen (or been forced) to live.

The trouble, however, is that those fears do not easily add up. As they descend one by one in a steady, though random succession, they defy our efforts (if efforts we make) to link them together and trace them to their joint roots. They are all the more frightening for being so difficult to comprehend; but even more horrifying for the feeling of impotence they arouse. Having failed to understand their origins and logic (if they do follow a logic), we are also in the dark and at a loss when it comes to taking precautions – not to mention preventing the dangers they signal or fighting back against them. We simply lack the tools and the skills. The dangers we fear transcend our ability to act; as yet we have not even advanced as far as to be able to conceive clearly what the tools and the skills adequate to the task would be like – let alone being able to start designing and creating them. We find ourselves in a situation not so different from that of a confused child; to use Georg Christoph Lichtenberg's allegory of three centuries ago, if a child hits a table because it knocked itself against it, 'we have instead for different but similar knocks devised the word Fate against which we utter accusations'.[23]

The feeling of impotence – that most frightening impact of fear – resides however not in the perceived or guessed threats as such, but in the vast yet abominably poorly furnished space stretching between the threats from which the fears emanate and our responses – those available and/or deemed realistic. Our fears 'do not add up' also in another sense: fears which haunt the many may be strikingly similar in each singular case, but it is presumed they will be fought back against individually, by each one of us using our own and in most cases sorely inadequate resources. More often than not, it is not immediately clear what our defence would gain by putting our resources together and seeking ways of giving all sufferers an equal chance of security from fear. To make things worse still: even when (if) the benefits of joint struggle are convincingly argued, the question remains of how to bring the solitary fighters together and how to keep them together. The conditions of individualized society are inhospitable to solidary action; they militate against seeing the forest behind the trees. Besides, old forests, once familiar and easily recognizable sights, have been decimated and new ones are unlikely to be established once land cultivation has tended to be subsidiarized to individual small-holding farmers. Individualized society is marked by a dissipation of social bonds, that foundation of solidary action. It is also notable for its resistance to a solidarity that could make social bonds durable – and reliable.

This book is a (very preliminary, incomplete) inventory of liquid modern fears. It is also an attempt (very preliminary, richer in questions than in answers) to seek their common sources and the obstacles that pile up on the road to their discovery, and find the ways of putting them out of action or rendering them harmless. This book, in other words, is but an invitation to think of acting, and to act, thoughtfully – not a book of recipes. Its sole purpose is to alert us to the awesomeness of the task which (knowingly or not, willingly or not) we are certain to be faced with through most of the current century, so that humanity can see it through and emerge at the end feeling more secure and self-confident than it felt at its start.

1

Dread of Death

It's 3 June 2005 today when I am sitting down to write; it would have been an ordinary day, hardly distinguishable from other days before and after, if not for one thing – it happens to be also Day Eight of the Sixth Edition of *Big Brother*, the very first of the long series of *Eviction* days. Such coincidence makes this day extra-ordinary: for many, this was a day of revelation, a day of libera-tion, or a day of absolution – depending on the side from which they look.

Revelation: what you suspected long ago, but hardly ever dared to think, and what you would have angrily denied all knowledge of if asked – now you watch on the screen, bathing in the glory of gigantic headlines splashed all over the tabloid front pages. And you do that in the company of millions of men and women like you. What you felt all along but would have been in trouble to put into words has now been spelled out for you, and for everybody else, in all its deliciously exciting and nauseatingly sinister clarity, and with an authority as irrepressible as only the stampeding mil-lions could bestow. To cut a long story short: you now *know*, and know for sure, what you merely *felt* (suspected, guessed) before.

This how the story on the 'official *Big Brother* site' went:

As Craig prepared for what could potentially be his final night's sleep in the *Big Brother* House, his thoughts were clearly on the impending eviction.

    While his Housemates were divided between sleeping in the bedroom and talking in the seating area, Craig chose to sit alone in the kitchen with only himself for company.

    Wearing his dressing gown, he cut a lonely figure as he sat alone in the kitchen slumped over the work surface. With his head in his hands a sad-looking Craig gazed around forlornly into space. He looked like a mere shadow of the bubbly boy who had dressed up as Britney to entertain his Housemates earlier in the evening. Obviously the idea that he could have just had his last full day in the House had got to him ... After a few minutes of more aimless staring and appearing totally lost in thought he finally decided to call it a night and took himself off to bed.

    Looking like a lost puppy, he was still unable to settle and sat up in bed looking into the darkness.

Poor Craig, the looming eviction has really got under his skin.

    'Impending eviction' ... 'The last full day' ... Having 'only himself for company' ... All that sounds so painfully familiar. Well, when you read that report, it seemed as if someone obligingly served you with a looking-glass. Or rather, if someone miraculously managed to plumb a TV camera, complete with mikes and spotlights, into the darkest corners of your mind where you've dreaded to visit ... Didn't you, like the rest of us, feel a Craig inside waiting to come out? Well, Craig did so, and we should all be grateful for the lesson his torments taught us. Never mind that the next day you'll learn that Craig's terrors were premature, and that it was Mary, not him, who got kicked out first.

    'Ladbrokes said Mary's popularity had "plummeted" after she refused to wear a microphone,' explains the official *Big Brother* website, quoting the *experts* who – being experts – *must* know best the things on which they are the experts; and the things about which the quoted experts knew best were the twists and turns of public sympathies and antipathies. It was his glib *loquacity* that was Craig's original sin that threatened him with being consigned to waste, as the experts said (and as a viewer, signed 'crash', complained in the name of thousands of like-minded viewers: 'He is an absolute disgrace: illiterate, insipid, fatuous, fat and stupid to boot. He adds nothing to the house. Get him out and then boot off his lapdog next') – but obviously Mary's *refusal* of public confession was found even more off-putting and condemnable than all Craig's faults put together. And when Mary finally gave up and made herself audible, she fell into yet deeper trouble: she 'kept criticising others' . . . On Thursday, she said: 'I want to leave. Everybody disgusts me. I'm not a wannabe. There is no intellectual conversation in here and I need it.'

So what is better? To keep your tongue, or to oblige the snoopers by spitting your inside out and laying your innermost thoughts on the table? There is evidently no good answer to that question. Heads you lose, tails they win. There is *no foolproof way to stave off your eviction*. Its threat won't go away. There is little, if anything, that you can do to make sure that the blow is diverted (or even postponed). No rules, no recipes. Just keep trying – and erring. And just in case you missed Day Eight's lesson: a mere seven days later, when on Day Fifteen it is Lesley's lot to be evicted from the House ('Lesley left the *Big Brother* House . . . to a tumultuous chorus of boos from the waiting crowd'), Craig's turn comes to fulminate against the inscrutable shifts of fate: 'It's ridiculous,' he sulks. 'I can't believe it. She has done nothing to deserve going.'

Well, the whole point is, isn't it, that one does *not* need 'to do something' 'to deserve' the eviction. Eviction has nothing to do with justice. When it comes to the crowd's choice between boos and cheers, the idea of 'just desserts' is neither here nor there (even if, when hunting with the hounds instead of running with the hare, you would rather deny that). You cannot be sure that the order to pack up and go is coming, and nothing you do will make it come or stop it coming.

What Reality TV reports is *fate*. For all you know, eviction is an *unavoidable* fate. Just like death, which you may try to keep at a distance for a while, but nothing you try can stop it when it finally strikes. This is how things are, and don't ask why . . .

Liberation: now that you know, and also know that your knowledge is shared by millions and that it comes from a source you can trust (not for nothing was 'audience opinion' selected as the lifeline for those seeking truth in *Who Wants to Be a Millionaire* – another highly popular TV show), you can stop tormenting yourself. There was no need to feel ashamed either of your feelings, suspicions and premonitions, or of your struggle to chase them out of your mind and consign them to rot in the darkest cellars of your subconscious. Were they not given and taken in public, Big Brother's commands, calculated to find out which of the House residents will fail first in their efforts to meet them, would be just like any other psychoanalytical session. Such sessions, after all, are meant to allow you to live happily ever after with thoughts which until yesterday seemed unendurable, and proudly parade today in what a mere few days ago would have looked like the garb of infamy. In that public psychoanalytical session called *Big Brother*, your cryptic premonitions have received resounding approval by no less an authority than Reality TV, and so you no longer need puzzle and torment yourself: this is indeed how the *real* world works. Today's Big Brother, unlike George Orwell's predecessor whose name he borrowed without asking, is not about keeping people *in* and making them stick to the line, but about kicking people *out* and making sure that once they are kicked out they will duly go and won't come back . . .

That world, as 'Reality TV' has vividly shown and convincingly proved, is all about 'who sends whom to the refuse tip'; or, rather, who'll do it *first*, while there is still time to do to the others what they would dearly wish, given the chance, to do to you – and *before* they manage to act on their wishes. You saw Mary saying, when still carrying a microphone, about someone else who was later to vote for *her* eviction: 'arrogant old man, he shouldn't be here!' Mary, about to be victimized, played the same game as the victimizers did, and did not play it differently; if allowed, she would not hesitate a second in joining in the hue and cry.

And, as you ought to have guessed, there is no way to repeal evictions altogether. The question is not *whether*, but *who* and *when*. People get being kicked out not because they are bad, but because it is in the rules of the game that someone *must* be evicted and because other people have proved to be more skilful in the art of out-manoeuvring others like them; that is, in out-playing other players in the game they all play, those who evict and those who are evicted alike. It is not that people keep being expelled because they are found to be unworthy of staying in the game. It is the other way round: people are declared unworthy of staying because there is a quota of evictions that needs to be met. One of the house residents *must* be expelled week in, week out – every week, whatever happens. These are house rules, obligatory for all house residents, however they might otherwise behave.

Big Brother is frank: there is nothing in the house rules about rewarding the virtuous and punishing the evildoers. It is all about the quota of weekly evictions that needs to be fulfilled come what may. You heard Davina McCall, the presenter, shouting: 'The fate of Craig and Mary is in your hands!' Meaning: there is a choice, and you are at liberty to choose your victim; you have a choice between expelling one *or* the other – but no choice of not expelling either or of letting both stay. So, from now on, once they have been resoundingly confirmed, feel free to follow your instincts and intuitions. You can't go wrong voting for someone's eviction. It's only when hesitating and resisting playing that you take the chance of staying or being stood out of the game. And your distaste for playing the game of exclusion won't stop the rest from blackballing you.

Finally – the *absolution*. A double, two-edged absolution, as a matter of fact: retrospective, and anticipatory. Indeed, old misdeeds and future craftiness are both now forgiven. The past gropings in the dark have been presently recycled into the wisdom of future rational choices. You have learned – but you've also been *trained*. With the revealed truth came useful skills, and with the liberation came the courage to put the skills into operation. For that official verdict of 'not guilty' you are grateful to the *Big Brother* producers. And it is out of that gratitude that you join the crowds glued to the screen – helping thereby to render the verdict authoritative, truly public and universally binding, and on the way raising sky-high TV ratings and profits . . .

Big Brother is a messy show, or at least, as the more benign critics would prefer to say, 'multifaceted' or 'multi-tiered'. There is something in it for everyone, or at least for many, perhaps for most – whatever their gender, skin hue, class or school certificate. The desperate struggle of the housemates to escape eviction might draw to TV screens the lovers of filth or people anxious to know how far down and how varied are the hidden depth's below those to which humans are commonly known to fall; it will pull in and keep enthralled the fans of bared flesh and of everything else saucy and sexy; it has quite a lot to offer to people in need of a richer vocabulary of foul language and of more object lessons in its usage. Indeed, the list of benefits is long and variegated. The devotees of *Big Brother* have been charged by their critics, each time with a sound reason, with any number of base motives.

Occasionally some noble ones have even been imputed to them too.

And so different people may switch over to the *Big Brother* show for different reasons. The main message of the show seeps in surreptitiously, wrapped in too many other attractions to be immediately and unerringly spotted; it may come unexpectedly and unbargained for to many viewers seeking other diversions; it may even stay unnoticed by some. As for the critics primarily concerned with the defence of good manners (and particularly with protecting their own inalienable and indivisible right to single out good taste from vulgarity), that main message may escape totally unnoticed . . .

It can't happen, though, in the case of *The Weakest Link* show – only thinly camouflaged as a knowledge-testing TV quiz and even more thinly as another prize-chase tournament, and offering the viewers no spiritual or carnal delights except the spectacle of human humiliation followed by eviction followed by self-immolation. Questions and answers, alas unavoidable in a show classified in the 'quiz' category, are proffered with a haste that betrays embarrassment and begs forgiveness: 'I am so terribly sorry to waste precious time that ought to have been devoted to the thing that truly counts – but you know as I know that you and I must keep up appearances'; questions and answers that are regrettable, even if unavoidable, interruptions of the main plot, brief intervals separating the successive lengthy acts of the drama – for some, if not most viewers, just occasions to relax and have another sip of tea and another crisp.

The Weakest Link is the message of *Big Brother* undiluted – a message pressed into a pill. As far as possible, it is stripped to the bare essentials and goes straight to the heart of the matter, that is to the celebration of the eviction routine. The players, left in no doubt that this is indeed the name of the game they play, are one by one evicted not in a matter of many long weeks, but in thirty minutes. Contrary to what its official name suggests, the real purpose unravelled in the course of the show is not to discover who are the 'weakest players' in successive rounds, but to remind everyone that in every round someone must be declared 'the weakest' and to demonstrate that the turn of everyone, except the single winner, to be proclaimed the weakest will inevitably arrive since all but one are bound to be eliminated. All but one are redundant before the game starts; the game is played only to reveal who is the one exempted from the common fate.

At the start of *The Weakest Link* show there is a team of several players, all contributing their wins to the shared kitty. In the end, there is just one player, pocketing all the spoils. Survival is the chance of one; damnation is the destiny of all the rest. Before they themselves are voted out, all playmates will partake in the successive extradition rituals, with a satisfaction only offered by a duty diligently performed, a job well done, or a lesson firmly learned, with possible pangs of conscience quelled by the proof that the misdeeds of the evicted neighbour made their verdict a foregone conclusion. After all, an integral (perhaps the main) part of the players' duty is to follow the voting-out ceremony with the admission of their own responsibility for defeat and a public confession of the shortcomings that invited ostracism and made the eviction both just and inevitable. The main deficiency confessed, and with monotonous regularity, is the sin of failing to outsmart the others . . .

Moral tales of yore were about the rewards awaiting the virtuous and the punishments prepared for the sinners. *Big Brother*, *The Weakest Link* and countless similar moral tales offered to, and avidly absorbed by the residents of our liquid modern world, hammer home other and different truths. First, punishment is the norm, reward is an exception: the winners are those who have been exempted from the universal sentence of eviction. Second, the links between virtue and sin on the one hand and rewards and punishments on the other are tenuous and haphazard. You may say: the Gospels reduced to the Book of Job . . .

What the moral tales of our times tell is that blows hit at random, needing no reason and commanding no explanation; that there is but the weakest (if any) link between what men and women do and what befalls them; and that there is little or nothing they can do to make sure that suffering will be avoided. 'Moral tales' of our times are about the iniquitous menace and the imminence of eviction, and about human near-impotence to stave off that fate.

All moral tales act through sowing fear. If, however, the fear sown by the moral tales of yore was redeeming (that fear came complete with an antidote: with a recipe for averting the fear-begetting threat, and so for a life free from fear), the 'moral tales' of our time tend to be unmerciful; they promise no redemption. The fears they sow are intractable and indeed *ineradicable*: they are here to stay – they can be suspended or forgotten (repressed) for a time, but not exorcised. For such fears no antidote has been found and none is likely to be invented. These fears penetrate and saturate the whole of life, reach every nook and cranny of body and mind and recast the life process into an uninterrupted and unfinishable 'hide-and-seek', 'bo-peep, peek-a-boo' game; a game in which a moment of inattention results in irredeemable defeat.

Those moral tales of our times are public rehearsals of death. Aldous Huxley imagined the Brave New World conditioning/ inoculating children against fear of death through treating them to their favourite sweets while they were gathered around the deathbeds of their elders. Our moral tales try to inoculate us against fear of death by banalizing the sight of dying. They are the daily dress rehearsals of death dressed up as social exclusion, hoping that before it arrives in its naked form we will get used to its banality.

Irreparable . . . Irremediable . . . Irreversible . . . Irrevocable . . . Beyond recall or remedy . . . The point of no return . . . The final . . . The ultimate . . . The *end* of *everything*. There is one and only one event to which all such qualifiers can be ascribed in full and with no exception; one event that renders all the other applications of such concepts metaphorical; the event that accords them with their primal meaning – pristine, unadulterated and undiluted. That event is *death*.

Death is fearful because of that quality unlike any other qualities; a quality of rendering all other qualities no longer negotiable. Each event we know or know of – *except death* – has a past as well as a future. Each event – except death – has a promise written in indelible ink, even if in the smallest of prints, that the plot is 'to be continued'. Death carries only one inscription: *Lasciate ogni speranza* (though Dante Alighieri's idea of engraving that final sentence from which there was no appeal over the gate to Hell was not really legitimate, since all sorts of things went on happening after crossing hell's gate . . . after that sign to 'Abandon all hope'). Only death means nothing will happen from now on, nothing will happen to *you*, that is – nothing will happen that *you* will be able to see, hear, touch, smell, enjoy or bewail. It is for that reason that death is bound to remain incomprehensible to the living; indeed, when it comes to drawing a truly impassable limit to human imagination, death has no competitors. The one and only thing we can't and never will be able to visualize is a world that does not contain us visualizing it.

No human experience, however rich, offers an inkling of how it feels when nothing is going to happen and nothing more is to be done. What we learn from life, day in day out, is exactly the opposite; but death annuls everything we've learned. Death is the 'unknown' incarnate; and among all other *unknowns* it is the only one fully and truly *unknowable*. Whatever we've done to prepare for death, death finds us unprepared. To add insult to injury, it makes the very idea of 'preparation' – that accumulation of knowledge and skills which defines life wisdom – null and void. All other cases of hopelessness and haplessness, ignorance and impotence could be, with due effort, cured. Not this one.

The 'original fear', the fear of death (an inborn, endemic fear), we, human beings, share it seems with all animals, owing to the survival instinct programmed in the course of evolution into all animal species (or at least into those among them which survived long enough and so left enough traces to have their existence recorded). But only we, human beings, know of death's inescapability and so face also the awesome task of surviving the acquisition of that knowledge; the task of living with the awareness of death's inevitability, and despite it. Maurice Blanchot went as far as to suggest that whereas man knows of death only because he is man – he is only man because he is a death in the process of becoming.[1]

The Sophists, who preached that fear of death is contrary to reason – arguing that when death is here I am here no longer, and when I am here, death is not – were wrong: whenever I am, I am in the company of my *awareness* that sooner or later death *must* put an end to my being here. In resolving this task, in fighting back or defusing that 'secondary fear' – the fear oozing not from death knocking on the door, but from our knowledge that it surely will, sooner or later – instincts, were we equipped with them, would be of little help. The resolution of that task must be undertaken and done, if it can be done at all, by human beings themselves. And it is done – for better or worse, though with but mixed success.

All human cultures can be decoded as ingenious contraptions calculated to make life with the awareness of mortality liveable.

The inventiveness of cultures in the field of 'making it possible to live with inevitability of death' is astonishing, though not boundless. In fact, the amazing variety of the stratagems on record can be reduced to a small number of categories; all their variants could be registered under a few essential strategies.

By far the most common and apparently the most effective, and so also the most tempting among the relevant cultural inventions, is denial of the finality of death: an (essentially untestable) idea that death is not the end of the world, but a passage from one world to another (as Sandra M. Gilbert recently put it[2] – an *expiration*, not the *termination*). The dying won't fall out of the only world that exists and dissolve and disappear in the netherworld of non-being, but will just move to another world – where they'll continue to exist, albeit in a somewhat different (though comfortingly similar) shape from the one they've become used to calling theirs. Corporeal existence may cease (or be merely suspended until the second coming, or the day of the last judgment, or shed one form only to enter another bodily form, as in the eternal return through reincarnation); used-up and worn-out bodies may disintegrate; but 'being in the world' is not confined to this fleshy/bony carapace here and now. Indeed, the current bodily existence may well be but a recurrent episode of a never-ending, though constantly form-changing existence (as in the case of reincarnation) – or an overture to an eternal life of soul that starts at death, turning thereby the moment of death into a moment of liberation of soul from its corporeal casing (as in the Christian vision of life after death).

The admonition *memento mori*, to remember death, which accompanies the proclamation of life's eternity testifies to the awesome potency of that promise to fight back against the incapacitating impact of death's imminence. Once the proclamation is heard, absorbed and believed, there is no longer any need to try (in vain, as it were!) to forget about death's inevitability. No need for eyes to be averted from its unavoidable arrival. Death is no longer the Gorgon whose very sight would kill: not only *can* one look death in its face, but *ought* to look it in the face day in day

out and twenty-four hours a day, lest one forgets to care about
the sort of new life imminent death will augur. Remembering the
imminence of death keeps the life of mortals on the right track –
by endowing it with a purpose that makes every lived moment
precious. 'Memento mori' means: live your earthly life in such a
way as to earn happiness in the life after death. Life after death
is guaranteed – indeed inescapable; its quality, however, depends
on how you live your life *before* you die. It may be a nightmare.
It may be bliss. And now to work . . .

The soul's eternity bestows on earthly life a truly priceless
value. It is only here and now, on earth, when the soul is still
enclosed in its fleshy carapace, that eternal bliss may be assured
and eternal torment staved off. Once the corporeal life ends, it
will be too late. The verdict, carrying 'no second chance', which
death is believed to portend has been given an altogether new
meaning – indeed reversed. If, once the opportunities to practise
virtue and eschew vice come to an end, as they must at the
moment of death, the choice between Heaven and Hell will already
have been made and the soul's fate decided – for eternity, then it
is precisely that abominably brief *earthly* life which holds the real
power over *eternity*; and the obligation of *memento mori* prods
the living to exercise that power.

The Christian concept of hereditary original sin was a particularly felicitous invention; it raised yet higher the value of bodily life
and magnified its significance. It rendered the chance of earning a
place in Heaven everything but fifty-fifty. With the odds set heavily
against their chance of a place in Heaven, the heirs of original sin
were prodded to be positive about their life tasks; since no one is
born innocent, but burdened from the very start with hereditary
sin, mortals need to be doubly earnest and zealous in exercising
their short-lived potency of earning salvation. Steering clear of evil
deeds won't be enough: in addition to good deeds, as many of them
as possible, self-sacrifice, self-immolation and self-administered
expiatory suffering are also called for to wash away the stigma of
original sin which the hellish fires would otherwise need an eternity
to burn out. The prospect of eternity was a nightmare for the evil
and the lackadaisical, but a source of perpetual joy for the good
and diligent. Each of its two faces inspired action.

Turning death around – recasting the most abhorrent of falls
as the most blissful of ascents – was a truly virtuoso move. Not

only did it manage to reconcile mortals to their mortality, but it invested life with a sense, purpose and value which the verdict of death would have emphatically denied if it had been left in its straightforward, stern simplicity. That move turned the destructive might of death into a formidable life-enhancing power: it harnessed death to the chariot of life. It brought eternity within reach of the transient, and put the self-acknowledged mortals at the controlling desk of immortality.

That act was hard to follow, though imitating it has been tried in all sorts of fashions and most certainly will never stop being tried. Hardly any replacement proved to be as radical as the original in taming and domesticating the spectre of death. Only the original presented life after death as the universal and non-negotiable destiny, thereby re-presenting the fear-inspired concern with death as a universal – and redeeming – duty. All imitations instead cast immortality as a 'life by proxy', and even in that severely diminished form as only a chance – something that could be grasped, but also missed. Individuals who struggled, however successfully, to grasp their chance of earning that substitute immortality did not get the promise of experiencing or even witnessing the effects of their victory in person. To those who asked why they should give up the delights they were able to experience for the sake of joys they could only imagine and would never witness, the surrogate propositions, unlike the original stratagem, were unable to offer a satisfactory, overwhelmingly (let alone universally) convincing answer.

However imperfect they might be, all the substitutes have been designed on the pattern of the life-after-death formula, trying to make mortal life meaningful by harping on the *durability of the effects* of an admittedly *transient* earthly life, to give reassurance that hard work performed in the course of that life won't be wasted, and so to convince doubters that the fashion in which one lives that life will matter long after life itself grinds to a halt, whereas nothing that happens later will be able to annul its consequences.

According to this formula, it is up to every mortal to decide whether or not his or her life should make a difference to the world that will persists after his or her death, and what kind of a difference it should be. That world which will persist after the expiry of one's own lifespan will be inhabited by others; the one who made the difference won't be among its residents; but the others who will be there will experience the impact of the life that ended – and hopefully acknowledge it. They will be grateful to those to whom they owe what they cherish and will see to it that they survive in their grateful memory. But even if they don't know the names of individuals whose deeds made their life different (better) from what it otherwise would have been, the fact remains that the life of someone mortal and by now forgotten bore fruit and left lasting traces.

By comparison with the original stratagem, its modified – surrogate – versions ostensibly multiplied the choices open to mortals. For those inspired by the chance of gaining the kind of immortality offered by the substitute versions, the range of choices was widened far beyond the single dilemma of Heaven and Hell. Once the prospect of immortality in whatever form stops being a foregone conclusion, a large space for invention and experiment is thrown open for all concerned. And once denial of the finality of death has been decoupled from the immortality of the soul, it is free to be dovetailed with any number of alternatives. And it has been – though again the impressive variety of cultural inventions can be roughly reduced to two classes: those offering a *personal* immortality; and those promising a personal contribution to the survival and perseverance of an *impersonal* entity, more often than not at the expense of playing down the importance of individual identity, and ultimately asking for a readiness for self-denial and self-effacement.

Individuality, as it happens, tends in all kinds of society to be a coveted, closely watched and guarded privilege of a few. To be an individual means to stand out from the crowd; to carry a recognizable face and be known by name; to avoid being confused with any other individuals and so preserving one's own *ipséité*. On the canvases portraying past 'historical moments' (that is, those moments believed to be worth recording because their consequences reached beyond their own time and changed the subsequent flow of affairs by leaving a tangible imprint on the present), you can set apart 'the individuals' from 'the crowd' or the 'mass' by, respectively, the unique and recognizable faces of the first and the seriality, vagueness or invisibility of faces of the second.

Such a sharp contrast should not be surprising; after all, individuality is a 'value' only in as far as it does not come as a 'free gift', only if it needs to be struggled for and requires an effort to be achieved – and for all such reasons is in principle available to some while staying stubbornly beyond the reach of the rest. Were there no faceless crowds – 'mob', 'herd', 'horde' or just 'rabble' – or were individuality an inborn, unproblematic, matter-of-fact quality of every and any person, the idea of the individual would surely lose much of its lustre and attraction, though in all probability it wouldn't have been born in the first place. Access to the means of preserving the recognizable uniqueness of face and name for the times to come, including the times that will follow their bearer's death, is a necessary attribute, but also perhaps the most desirable ingredient, of 'individuality'.

The principal means to achieve such an effect is 'fame', a shorthand for 'being kept in the memory of posterity'. Paradoxically for a vehicle of individual immortality, it is membership of a *category* that ensures access to fame, and the fight for such access (including the fight to make a category eligible for bestowing such immortality on its members) has been throughout history a collective affair. Initially a prerogative of kings and generals, eligibility was subsequently won by statesmen and revolutionaries (and obliquely by the scandalizers and rebels, their distorting-mirror replicas), by discoverers and inventors, scientists and artists. Dynastic regimes had their own rules of fame distribution, as had theocracies, republics and democracies; agrarian and industrial societies; premodern, modern and postmodern cultures.

Let us note, though, that the collectively or categorially sustained right to individual fame is a double-edged sword; it may feel like a cruelty of fate rather than a stroke of good fortune. The institutionally ensured right to individual fame does not guarantee that the right kind of fame, the *glory*, will be allocated; it may mean in practice an eternity of infamy. All memory, including the memory of posterity, is a mixed blessing. If you belong to a social category that endows individual performances, whether approved or condemned, with the prospect of being recorded and commemorated – fame is a *fate*; but this fame's capacity of survival, and its contents, stay perpetually and vexingly underdefined. The right to individual fame rebounds as a duty of incessant effort and undying vigilance – just as the right to salvation called for lifelong, never-lapsing goodness. It promises no rest and portends a life full of anxiety, self-critique and possibly self-reprobation. Missing or misusing a chance may taste no less, if not more bitter than its denial.

For those to whom the chance of individual immortality has been denied – for the faceless, anonymous *hoi polloi*, the 'ordinary', 'undistinguished' men and women, that raw stuff of which statistical tables are made – another variant of immortality is on offer: immortality-by-proxy, or immortality-through-the-surrender-of-individuality. Or other *variants* rather, considering how many versions of such depersonalized immortality have been and are on offer, each capitalizing in its own way on the unhealed and ultimately incurable fear of the Great Unknown.

Personalized immortality is a life-enhancing proposition, calling for hard efforts to 'leave a trace': to perform memorable deeds. Depersonalized immortality does just the opposite. It is offered, as a consolation prize, to those many – innumerable – men and women who have little hope of accomplishing anything counted as significant and so also have meagre prospects of gaining a secure place in human memory on their own. Impersonal immortality compensates for personal impotence; anonymous existence is given a chance of (also anonymous) eternity. Yes, their own lives will be forgotten, but they will still make a difference – they won't pass without trace. What will make that difference, however, and what will engrave deep traces on the infinite duration, is the way they *die*. Unable to earn immortality through *life*, they will still earn it through *death*; that would make their death instrumental in bringing forth something much more solid, lasting, trustworthy and significant than their uneventful, drab and unprepossessing individual life deprived of the chance of making their presence felt and noted as long as they lived. It is through the survival of that 'something' that they themselves may achieve immortality by proxy – by making their death an offering to a (hopefully undying) *cause*.

At the threshold of the nation-building era, the post-revolutionary French Republic resurrected the ancient Roman formula *pro patria*, and so set a pattern for this 'immortality by proxy', the 'compensatory immortality'. It achieved it through what George L. Mosse called the 'nationalization of death'[3] – a strategy to be followed throughout the modern times.

The budding/aspiring nations needed state powers to feel secure, and the emergent state needed national patriotism to feel powerful. Each needed the other to survive. The state needed subjects of the state as patriots of the nation, ready to sacrifice their individual lives for the sake of the survival of the nation's 'imagined community'; the nation needed its members as subjects of a state empowered to conscript them to the 'national cause' and, in case of need, to force them to surrender their lives in the service of the nation's immortality. Both the state and the nation found the most fitting solution to their respective problems in the idea of an *anonymous* death leading to *impersonal* immortality.

In the era of mass conscript armies and universal military duty, the untapped horror of death and the fear of the void to which death was suspected to lead were profitably deployed in the mobilization of mass patriotism and dedication to the national cause. As Mosse points out, whereas 'the death in war of a brother, husband or friend' continued to be seen as a 'martyr death' – a personal sacrifice – 'now, at least in public, the gain was said to outweigh the personal loss'. The death of the national hero could be a personal loss and tragedy, but the sacrifice was amply rewarded, though not by the salvation of the immortal *soul* of the dying, but by the bodily immortality of the nation. Monuments to the fallen, scattered all over Europe, reminded passers-by that the grateful nation repaid the sacrifice of its sons with never-fading memory of their service; and that the nation wouldn't live to erect the monuments in honour of the dead were it not for the willing sacrifice of their lives.

Memorials designed in the capitals of Europe celebrated the unselfishness of Unknown Soldiers and hammered home the idea that neither the military rank of the heroes nor indeed their whole life lived until the moment of the ultimate sacrifice mattered for that sacrifice to be appreciated and fondly remembered. Those memorials let the living know that only the moment of death on the battlefield counted, and that the *worthiness of the death* had the power to retrospectively redefine (elevate and ennoble) the meaning of even an *unworthiest of lives*. The annual public displays of national memory served an additional purpose. They reminded viewers and the participants in anniversary ceremonies that the longevity of the posthumous existence in the memory of posterity depends on the continuous existence of the nation:

sacrifice is to be remembered as long as (but no longer than) the nation lives – and so the sacrifice of personal life for the nation's survival is not just the way to transcend death, but also the condition of a universe into which the posthumous existence can be transplanted, flourish and feel secure . . .

The stratagem first deployed by the spokesmen for up-and-coming nations set a pattern that the promoters of numerous other causes tried, seldom completely successfully, to emulate; not so much perhaps for its potential to heal the wounds inflicted by the horror of the finality of death (that potential was debatable at all times), as thanks to the wondrous opportunity to redeploy the inextinguishable fear of the void-after-death in the service of causes they wished to advance or save. The formula of 'you'll die, yet thanks to your death the cause served by your death will live forever – and so will render the immortality of your feat even more secure than any number of monuments carved in stone or cast in steel' was particularly keenly exploited by revolutionary movements that promoted a thorough and lasting overhaul of the social order following the pattern of nation-building, though hardly ever to similarly weighty effect.

However sharp the differences between them, the means of personal and impersonal immortality alike recognize the gravity of the problem with which the non-negotiable finality of death confronts all humans as beings aware of their mortality. Such means, their popularity and (at least partial) effectiveness obliquely testify to the important place occupied by the worry about eternal life (or its denial) among the concerns of mortals. They are, so to speak, roundabout tributes (or ransoms?) to the awesome, sublime, definitely *super*human and so terrifying power of eternity, paid by humans all too aware of their own life's brevity. And they 'make sense' only on condition that the terror of death continues, that the propitiatory tribute is willingly offered and the ransom required is commonly willed to be paid.

One more cultural stratagem runs parallel to the family of expedients thus far surveyed. As the historically shaped conditions of the efficacity (and so of the attractiveness) of the above discussed expedients begin to dissolve and disappear, this alternative stratagem, gradually yet steadily gathering force and popularity throughout the modern era, seems to be acquiring pride of place in our liquid modern society of consumers. This stratagem consists in the *marginalization* of concerns with finality, through the devaluation of anything durable, long-lasting, long term; the devaluation of anything likely to outlive individual life or even the fixed-term pursuits into which the span of life is split, but also of such life experiences as provide the stuff of which the idea of eternity is moulded to prompt the worry about one's place in it.

The stratagem of marginalization consists in a systematic effort to evict the worry about eternity (and, indeed, about duration as such) from human consciousness and strip it of its powers to dominate, shape and streamline the course of individual life. Instead of promising bridges connecting mortal life to eternity, that alternative stratagem openly plays down, degrades or refutes the value of duration, cutting all concerns with immortality at their roots; it transplants the importance once allocated to the 'thereafter' onto the present moment; from the durable to the transient. It thereby decouples the horror of death from its original cause, rendering it amenable to other uses, boasting effects more tangible and (above all) immediate than concerns with life after death.

There are two essential ways in which this can be attained. One is the *deconstruction* of death. Another is its *banalization*.

Having observed that 'we showed an unmistakable tendency to put death on one side, to eliminate it from life', Sigmund Freud explains: 'Our habit is to lay stress on the fortuitous causation of the death – accident, disease, infection, advanced age; in this way we betray the effort to reduce death from a necessity to a chance.'[4] Such 'reduction' (or, to deploy a post-Freudian and somewhat more precise linguistic novelty, the 'deconstruction') of death is in tune with the spirit of modernity (note that Freud wrote the quoted words at a time when the modern spirit was at its boldest – because yet ignorant of its own limitations). It was a typically modern gesture to slice existential challenge into an aggregate of problems which need be resolved one by one and each on its own, and *can* be resolved in such a fashion providing that the know-how and the technical means necessary to use that know-how are available, and that the regime of its use is duly observed.

Somewhere in the background of the deconstructive urge loomed a vague and seldom articulated presumption that the quantity of problems already encountered and yet to be revealed is finite, and so the list of tasks still to be performed can be sooner or later fully run through and exhausted. It was hoped that even the grandest and most overwhelming of tasks, seemingly beyond human power to resolve since impossible to tackle in its entirety and to confront point-blank, could be dissected into a multitude of specific and individually soluble mini-tasks, and thereafter removed from the agenda – just as an empty shelf is disposed of once the whole of its contents have been gutted. It is not easy to demonstrate the futility of such a hope, since the long series of successful campaigns might effectively hide from view the unwin-nability of the war in whose name all those campaigns were launched and carried through.

What is hidden from view when deconstruction is applied to the issue of death is the hard and intractable fact of the biologi-cally determined mortality of human beings. One hears seldom, if at all, about humans dying of mortality . . . Even the notion of 'death by natural causes' – already a sanitized, euphemistic verbal substitute for 'mortality' – has fallen out of the vernacular. Medics will hardly ever record 'natural causes' when filling in the death certificate; if they lack an alternative, more specific explanation, they will certainly recommend a post-mortem to establish the 'genuine' (that is, immediate) cause of death. Their inability to locate such a cause would be decried as testimony of professional ineptitude. A specific cause of every single death must be pin-pointed and spelled out, and only such a reason to die may be accepted as a legitimate cause, which either *is* preventable or with due effort (that is, further research and development of medicines and procedures) can be *made* preventable – in principle at least, if not in every practical case. Neither the kin nor the friends of the deceased would take 'natural causes' as an explanation of why the death had occurred.

Such tactics, let us observe, are a fashion of myth-making exactly opposite to the strategy of representing history as nature, described in detail by Roland Barthes. The myth of the contin-gency of death is construed and sustained by representing a natural act as the product of so many human failures that could be avoided or ought to be rendered avoidable. Against Barthes's culture masquerading as nature, the naturalness of death is cam-ouflaged as culture. But then the function of the myths investi-gated by Barthes was to protect the brittle and contingent body of culture behind the shelter of the 'tremendous' – whereas the purpose of deconstructing death is precisely the opposite: stripping death of the aura of the tremendous it always and already carries.

If the prospect of immortality emphasizes the (instrumental) significance and the potency of mortal life while acknowledging the imminence of corporeal death, the deconstruction of death, paradoxically, intensifies the volume of the terror of death and drastically raises death's destructive potency even while ostensibly questioning its imminence. Instead of suppressing the awareness of the death's inevitability (its alleged effect) and freeing life pursuits from its pressure, it renders death's presence in life more ubiquitous and consequential than ever.

Death is now a permanent, invisible yet watchful and closely watched presence in every human undertaking, deeply felt, twenty-four hours a day and seven days a week. The memory of death is an integral part of any of life's functions. It is accorded high, perhaps the foremost authority whenever a choice is to be made in a life made of choices.

Once the terrifying worry of ultimate, yet distant death had been split into day in, day out worry about spying out in time and fighting back against (or better still warding off) the innumerable and ubiquitous singular and close-at-hand causes of death, and as alarms about newly discovered but heretofore unknown pathogenic substances and regimes follow one another in rapid succession, every act and every setting of action, including acts and settings thus far believed to be innocuous and harmless or not thought of at all as 'death relevant', become suspected of causing irreparable harm and bearing terminal consequences. From the threat of death there is now not a moment of rest. The fight against death starts from birth and fills the whole of life. As long as it goes on, it is punctuated with victories – even though the last battle is bound to be lost. Before that last battle, however (and who knows in advance which of the battles will transpire to be the last?), death stays 'hidden in the light'. Split into countless worries about uncountable threats, fear of death saturates the whole of life, though in the diluted form of a somewhat reduced toxicity. Thanks to the ubiquity of its small doses, the dread of death is unlikely to be 'taken in' whole and confronted in all its nightmarish ghastliness, and is commonplace enough to be unlikely to paralyze the will to live.

Hand in hand with deconstruction comes therefore the banalization of death, its indispensable but also inevitable companion. If deconstruction replaces one irresistible challenge with a multitude of commonplace and essentially fulfillable tasks, thereby hoping to avoid confrontation with the whole of its singular, ultimate horror, banalization makes that confrontation itself into a commonplace, almost a daily event, hoping thereby to make 'living with death' somewhat less unendurable. Banalization brings the one-off experience of death, by its nature inaccessible to the living, within the realm of mortals' daily routine, transforming their lives into perpetual rehearsals of death, and hoping thereby to familiarize them with the experience of 'finality' and thus to mitigate the horror oozing from the 'absolute alterity' – the total, absolute unknowability of death.

It is death that gives the idea of 'finality' its intelligible meaning, all other vernacular uses of the term being but direct or oblique references to that meaning. Representations of deaths are demonstrations of what that 'finality' – which otherwise would remain incomprehensible to us, the inveterate 'men hoping' (as Ernst Bloch insisted) – really means.

Jacques Derrida observed that each death is the end of *a world*, and each time the end of a *unique* world, a world that can never again reappear or be resurrected.[5] Each death is *a loss* of a world – a loss *forever*, an *irreversible* and *irreparable* loss. It is the *absence* of that world that will never end – being, from now on, eternal. It is through the shock of death, and the absence that follows it, that the meaning of finality, as much as the meanings of eternity, of uniqueness, of individuality in its twin facets of *la memêté* and *l'ipséité*, are revealed to us, mortals.

But as Vladimir Jankélévitch observed, not every death carries the same potency of revelation, enlightenment and instruction.[6] My own death cannot be comprehended as finality, nor imagined as such (I can't imagine the world from which I am absent without imagining my own presence in it as its witness, cameraman and reporter). The cessation of 'third persons' (strangers, the faceless and anonymous 'others'), which is bound to remain an abstract, demographic/statistical notion however large the figures in which it is expressed, is not going to strike us as an irreparable loss; when hearing of such a death we cannot refer that news to anything in particular that we may be losing (in Derrida's terms we may say that we did not know those worlds of whose disappearance we have been informed). All humans are mortal, we are used to the idea that all living species renew themselves through the mortality of all their members, and we assume, even if only implicitly, that given time the gaps laid open by death will be refilled; that loss, however great the numbers, is not irreparable.

And so it is only one kind of death, the death of 'thou', of the 'second' not a 'third', of the near and dear, of someone whose life intertwined with mine, that paves the ground for a 'privileged philosophical experience', since it offers me an inkling of that *finality* and *irrevocability* which death, every and any death, and *only* death, is about. Something irreversible and irreparable happens to me, something akin in this respect to my own death, even if this death of another is not yet my own. Sigmund Freud would concur: he noted the

> complete collapse when death struck down someone whom we love – a parent or a partner in marriage, a brother or sister, a child or a close friend. Our hopes, our desires and our pleasures lie in the grave with him, we will not be consoled, we will not fill the lost one's place.[7]

The last two paragraphs have spoken of a human, all too human predicament – universal and timeless. In all epochs and all cultures men's and women's lives tend to be intertwined with the lives of other humans – their kin, neighbours, close friends – just as our lives are. To some human beings around we are linked by the strings of sympathy and intimacy from which 'I–Thou' relationships are woven. Those selected others happen however to die, disappearing one by one from our world and carrying their own worlds with them into non-existence; in most cases they are not replaced, and in no case are they replaced completely – and this impossibility of fully replacing them offers an insight into the true meaning of 'uniqueness' and 'finality', enabling us to antici-pate the meaning of our own death even if we are still unable to visualize the world without our presence, the-world-after-our-own-death, the world without us watching it. As they leave one by one – our own worlds, the worlds of the survivors, bit by bit lose their contents. Those who have lived long and have seen many of their near and dear go, complain of the rising tide of loneliness: the eerie, uncanny experience of the world's emptiness – another oblique insight into the meaning of death.

For all such reasons, the end of an 'I–Thou' world sharing brought about by the demise of a companion-in-life may be, with only a minimum of simplification, described as a death experience 'once removed' (and let me repeat: this is the sole modality in which the experience of death is accessible by the living). But a similar end to the shared 'I–Thou' world may be caused by something other than the physical death of a close companion. Though brought about by different reasons, a breakdown of a relationship cutting an interhuman bond also carries a stamp of 'finality' (even if, unlike real death, that stamp may yet be wiped out; a relationship can be, theoretically speaking, re-enacted and so resurrected, even if the assumed likelihood of this happening tends to be severely diminished by the possibility of reconciliation being stubbornly denied and declared inconceivable in the heat of the estrangement of the partners); it could therefore be viewed as, so to speak, the death experience *twice* removed.

Death itself is 'banalized' by proxy when that second-order substitute, the 'twice-removed' death experience, turns into a frequently repeated and infinitely repeatable occurrence. This indeed happens when human bonds become fragile, tied together only provisionally, with little if any prospect of durability, and are from the start frightfully easy to untie at will and with little or no warning. As the human bonds of the liquid modern era become clearly brittle and 'until further notice', life turns into a daily rehearsal of death and of 'life after death', of resurrection or reincarnation – all performed by proxy, but like 'Reality TV' no less 'real' for that reason. The 'absolute alterity' that sets the death experience apart from all life experiences now becomes a familiar feature of quotidianity; stripped thereby of its mystery, familiarized and domesticated, the wild beast turns into a house pet.

Divorce may be but a simulacrum of widowhood – but, as Jean Baudrillard has pointed out, 'simulacrum' is not simulation,[8] which 'feigns' the features of reality and thereby inadvertently reinstates and reconfirms that reality's supremacy. Unlike simulation, 'simulacrum' denies the difference between reality and its representation, and so renders null and void the opposition between truth and falsity, or between the likeness and its distortion. Baudrillard compares simulacrum to psychosomatic illness, where it is futile to inquire whether the patient is 'really' ill or not, and even more hopeless to attempt to prove the patient's deception, since all the symptoms of the disease are present and look and feel exactly as the 'real stuff' would look and feel.

Frailty of human bonds is a prominent, indeed the defining attribute of liquid modern life. The blatant fissiparousness of human bonds and the frequency with which they are broken serves as a constant reminder of the mortality of human life. There is little point in questioning the validity of equating the loss of a partner due to separation with the 'truly final' loss caused by physical death; what counts, is that in *both* cases *'a* world', *each* time 'unique', vanishes – and that either the will or hope are missing to challenge, let alone reverse, the finality of its disappearance.

The vanishing of a companion-in-life may be but a metaphor of Jankélévitch's 'thou-death', but it is a metaphor that tends to be hardly distinguishable from what it stands for. And so is the aftermath of the break-up, devoted to weaving new ties, admittedly destined to be cut again just as the past bonds were. Death-by-proxy becomes an indispensable and constant link holding together the interminable sequence of 'new beginnings' and efforts to be 'born again', those characteristic features of liquid modern life, and a necessary stage in each one of the infinitely long series of the 'dying–being reborn–dying' cycles. In the ongoing drama of liquid modern life, death is one of the principal characters in the cast, reappearing in every act.

As an actor cast in the drama of liquid modern life, death differs however in a number of vital respects from the original to which it remains metaphorically locked – a circumstance that cannot but transform the way death is thought of and feared.

One of the most seminal among those respects is the decoupling of the idea of death from concerns with eternity. Death has been incorporated in the flow of life; no longer being the irrevocable end of life, it has become its integral (and possibly indispensable) part. There is no interface separating death from and connecting it to eternity. Death is not thought of as a passage from the transient to the eternal; nor is it contemplated as a gateway leading to immortality. Time before and after the experience of death 'twice removed' is similarly fragmented and discontinuous, and however painful the experience of the loss of a unique world might be, it was neither expected nor desired to lead into a different rhythm; it will not slow down the flow of episodes, let alone cause it to grind to a halt and be arrested altogether. In a liquid modern life there are no points of no return, and any prospect of such points would be shunned and actively (often successfully) resisted.

Mortality gleaned in the fragility and fissiparousness of human bonds differs starkly from that arising from the inborn frailty of human bodies.

In 'normal', 'peaceful' times, physical death is expected to come, with only relatively few (dubbed as 'abnormal', 'extraordinary', 'freak' or criminal) exceptions, as a result of the incapacity of the body to stay alive – of the body reaching its 'natural limit', the moment of 'euthanasia' as defined by Schopenhauer, or undergoing a pathological degradation like cancer; or as a result of interference from some known or as yet undiscovered but alien agents like contagious diseases, pollution, natural disasters, climate vagaries, passive smoking, etc., none of them intentionally caused by human actions.

The experience of a 'twice-removed' death, prompted by the breakage of human bonds, is however caused by humans – in each case an *intended* product of a deliberate, *purposeful* action. Sometimes it can be traced to an act that with a modicum of stretching could be registered under the rubric of (metaphoric) murder, but in most cases it is close to being classified as a result of (metaphoric) homicide. Behind every metaphorical death, human actors lurk, whether or not malice aforethought could be established and proven in court. Breaking a bond may happen 'by mutual consent', but seldom, if ever, does it result from the wishes of all who are involved and affected by its consequences, and equally seldom is it approved by them all. The event of breaking a bond divides partners into *perpetrators* and their *victims* (our 'culture of victimage and compensation', another defining characteristic of liquid modern life, can be traced to that circumstance). What is greeted by one side as a welcome act of liberation is perceived and lived by another as an abominable act of rejection and/or exclusion; an act of cruelty, undeserved punishment, or at best a proof of heartlessness.

Accordingly, the fear of a metaphorical 'twice-removed death' is at bottom the horror of being *excluded*. Saturated as it is with metaphorical deaths, liquid modern life is a life of undying suspicion and unrelenting vigilance. There is no way of knowing from which side of the bond the blow will come; who will be the first to deliver it, having tired of irksome commitments and promises of a loyalty that is hard to deliver, or having spotted more promising and less cumbersome attachments elsewhere; and who will prove to be sufficiently tough, bold and callous to declare the end of the relationship, to show the door or shut it behind the other, hang up the 'phone or stop answering calls.

Even if for different reasons, metaphorical death is as intractable, as difficult and often as impossible to avert as its archetype. There is no immunity – and there is no effective way for you to claim, let alone vindicate your rights, because there are no universally acknowledged rules to be invoked, or 'musts' and 'must nots' safely grounded in common beliefs and efficiently promoted by common practices, which you could turn to in order to convincingly prove that the verdict of exclusion – *your* 'metaphorical death' – has been unwarranted and the verdict ought to be quashed. There is no foolproof way of winning your case, however keenly you may try, and however earnestly you do.

Just the contrary. In a liquid modern setting, which happens to be also the setting of the society of consumers,[9] it is the personal and the individual, previously known as the 'intimate', that becomes 'political' (in Anthony Giddens's 'life politics' sense). This is, at any rate, what individual men and women are told, nudged or forced to believe – and to behave accordingly. They are prompted to design and then to play solo, each one on his or her own, all the legislative, executive and juridical instruments of the life politics symphony. In the individual courts of justice, the defendant, the jury and the judge are rolled into one person, who also writes down their own code of ad hoc procedural rules while sitting in judgment. There are no universally binding rules to which all individual courts are obliged to refer, or to which they could credibly and authoritatively resort. Sentences may be protested – but inevitably in another, similarly individual court of law, which may proceed by quite different rules and be guided by other principles. What in one individual court passes for just, may be rejected by another as a gross travesty of justice, whereas the common ground between the courts is much too shifty and volatile, and communication too perfunctory and accidental, for their disagreements to be settled and a decision be reached that would truly satisfy them both.

The dispute between individual judgments (if it comes to it, that is – if none of the sides boycotts the debating chamber, believing the case to be shut before it was opened, expecting no beneficial solution, or refusing *a priori* to acknowledge the authority of any court 'out there') tends therefore to be reduced to a force-and-obstinacy contest. The winners are those with more muscle and endurance power and less willingness to listen – but the losers are loath to admit the winners' victory; if they throw in the towel and lay down their weapons, they do it only for a time, waiting for the balance of forces to turn in their favour. What the losers learn from their defeat is that popular beliefs are correct when they insist that might is right, and that victories are proofs of greater strength and fewer scruples, not of greater wisdom and more justice, while defeats result from the inadvisable moral inhibitions and scruples of the defeated.

The modern spirit was born under the sign of the pursuit of happiness – of greater happiness and ever greater happiness. In the liquid modern society of consumers, each individual member is instructed, trained and groomed to pursue individual happiness by individual means and through individual efforts.

Whatever else happiness may mean, it always means freedom from inconvenience; and among the modern meanings of the concept of 'inconvenient', the Oxford English Dictionary lists 'not agreeing', 'unsuitable, inappropriate, out of place', 'unfavourable to comfort', 'incommodious, embarrassing, disadvantageous, awkward'. You can easily name (who can't?) quite a few individuals whom – as far as you are concerned – all such qualifiers fit like a glove. And they fit such people because those individuals stand in the way of *your* pursuit of *your* individual happiness. Can you name any reason why should you abstain from trying to evict those individuals, clearly 'out of place', from the place they are in?

Liquid modern life is lived on a battlefield. Pity the grass if
elephants choose it for their battleground – the field will be thickly
covered with 'collateral casualties' (be it the employees of companies falling victim to 'aggressive mergers', or children 'metaphorically orphaned' by divorced parents). But pity the elephants
battling on quicksand . . .

All liquid modern victories are, let me repeat, temporary. The
security they offer won't outlast the current balance of power,
which is expected to be as short-lived as all balances: just as
momentary snapshots of things on the move are known to be.
Dangers might have been pushed underground, but they have not
been and cannot be truly uprooted. And the shifting balance of
power, the only ground on which the volatile feeling of security
may rest, needs to be tested day in, day out, so that the slightest
symptoms of another shift may be spotted in time and – hopefully
– thwarted.

On the battlefield of liquid modern life, reconnaissance skirmishes, aimed at updating the inventory of threats and opportunities, never die down. A momentary lapse of vigilance will suffice
for the excluding to be excluded. A spectre hovers over that battlefield: the spectre of exclusion, of *metaphorical death.*

We have surveyed briefly the three essential strategies aimed at
making liveable a living-with-the-knowledge-of-the-imminence-
of-death. The first consists of building bridges between mortal life
and eternity – recasting death as a new beginning (this time of an
immortal life), rather than the end of ends. The second strategy
consists of shifting attention (and worry!) from death itself, as a
universal and inescapable event, to the specific 'causes' of death,
which are to be neutralized or resisted. And the third consists of
a daily 'metaphorical rehearsal' of death in its gruesome truth of
the 'absolute', 'ultimate', 'irreparable' and 'irreversible' end – so
that such an 'end', as in the case of 'retro' fads and fashions, can
come to be viewed as considerably less than absolute; as revocable
and reversible, just one more banal event among so many
others.

I am not suggesting that any of these strategies, or even all of
them applied together, are fully effective (they can't be, they are
but subterfuges and palliatives after all), or that they are free from
undesirable, and sometimes quite noxious, side-effects. But they

go some way towards taking the poison out of the sting and so allowing the unendurable to be endured by taming, and domesticating in the lived world-of-being, the 'absolute alterity' of non-being.

Let me also repeat that though we, human beings, share with animals the awareness of death *approaching*, and the panic fear such knowledge causes, only we, humans, know long before it strikes (indeed, from very beginning of our conscious life) that death is *inevitable*; that we are all, with *no exception*, mortal. We, and only we among sentient beings, have to live all our life with that knowledge. And only we have given death a name – setting in train a virtually infinite cavalcade of consequences which prove to be as inevitable as they were (and still are) unanticipated.

Jean Starobinski, having quoted La Rochefoucauld's observation that 'people would never fall in love if they did not hear love being talked about', and having thoroughly scanned the social history of human diseases, found out that 'there are illnesses (particularly neural and "moral" ones, neuroses and psychoses) which spread through being spoken of', with 'the word playing the role of the contaminating agent', and concluded that 'the verbalization enters the composition of the very structure of the lived experience' (*vécu*).[10] While Robert Bellah, discussing the recent spectacular rise of the American 'religious right', supplies the latest confirmation of the astonishing facility with which a free-floating signifier, complete with the emotions it evokes, may be used in such 'verbalization' by being reassigned to the signifieds chosen for their political convenience – even if neither materially nor logically is that emotion-loaded signifier related to the original objects responsible for raising the emotions in question.

> (T)he rise of the Religious Right correlates with the first wave of the impact of globalization on American society. Many American men that are pulled to the Religious Right are people who have lost their well-paying labour union jobs which had health care and retirement, and are now working low-end-jobs. And now their wives are working and sometimes their wives are making more money that they are making. Their whole sense of the meaning of life is coming down around their ears, and it's not because of gays and feminists. It's because of globalization. But the Republicans, with their tremendous propaganda machine, are able to turn this

alienation, which is rooted in structural changes in the American economy, into a cultural war . . .[11]

a war against gays and lesbians and feminists that is, and against the liberals who protect them and allow a sapping and eroding of the 'family values' remembered by the proud and confident bread-winners of yore now forced to rely on their wives' earnings or to face indigence, and by the secure and self-assured owners of jobs-for-life now stripped of their unionist shelter and exposed to the risks and humiliations of the 'flexible labour market'. All this happens in spite of the fact that the Republicans make no promises to strike at the root of those troubles; instead, they promote the kind of economic policy by which the families of most of those religious conservatives and evangelicals will be made to suffer a yet deeper, more painful and prospectless misery, instead of being helped.

Once settled in public imagery, a signifier can be detached from its signified, set floating and be reattached metaphorically or metonymically to an indefinite number of signifieds.

The particular signifier we are considering – 'death' – is in this respect uniquely, uncannily potent. Partly because it is ambivalence incarnate: the imminence of death fills life to the brim with primal fear (it was to make such fear intelligible, one may argue, that the aetiological myth of Adam and Eve's original sin was composed), but it acts as well, at least *in potentia*, as a most powerful stimulant. In other words, it endows life with enormous significance (in Hans Jonas's words, it makes days count and us count them) while simultaneously robbing that life of meaning. Such remarkable potency is seductive to all seekers of thunders available for stealing and redeployment; and so it tends to be keenly manipulated for all sorts of purposes.

The prohibition on pronouncing the true name of God (and the advice to avoid calling Satan by name, lest the sleeping dog be woken) being a fundamental rule of relating to 'the tremendous', and death being the archetype of the tremendous, looking death in its bare face is all but unbearable (the death-carrying Gorgon was a mythically recycled version of that unbearability). This is why manipulation can bring huge profits, and contains few if any risks: it can count on a grateful clientele among the millions trying desperately to avert their eyes from Gorgon's face.

Manipulation as such, in one form or another, is apparently inescapable. All cultures can be viewed as ingenious contraptions meant to mask and/or adorn that face and so make it 'lookable at' and 'liveable with' – but neither politics nor economy are slow to spot the chance and grasp it. Temptation is difficult to resist, as the manipulation comes relatively easily to all who are eager to try it for profit: they can count on the loyal support of human beings' aversion to standing still and doing nothing when they are confronted by a menace, on their proclivity to do something rather than nothing however negligible the effects of doing a particular something might be, and the human preference for simple tasks with clear and near targets over complex and opaque efforts with distant and misty objectives.

The phenomenon to be manipulated and capitalized on is the *fear of death* – one 'natural resource' that can boast infinite supplies and complete renewability. However ingenious the stratagems aimed at exorcising the phantom of death from the mind, the fear of death as such, be it in a reduced, reshaped or relocated form, cannot be chased away from human life. The primal fear of death is perhaps the prototype or archetype of all fears; the ultimate fear from which all other fears borrow their meanings. Dangers are conceived as 'threats' and derive their frightening power from the meta-danger of death – though they differ from the original by being avoidable and perhaps able to be prevented or even postponed indefinitely. Or so at least one may hope is the case, even if such hopes are frustrated more often than they are corroborated and upheld.

To quote Freud again:

> We are threatened with suffering from three directions: from our own body, which is doomed to decay and dissolution and which cannot even do without pain and anxiety as warning signals; from the external world, which may rage against us with overwhelming and merciless forces of destruction; and finally from our relations to other men. The suffering which comes from this last source is perhaps more painful than any other. We tend to regard it as a kind of gratuitous addition, although it cannot be any less fatefully inevitable than the suffering which comes from elsewhere.[12]

Threats attack from three directions, but all three marching columns aim at the same destination: the pain and suffering of the mortal body, experiences that are most harrowing in their own right for the distress and anguish they cause, but also mortifying – as dress rehearsals of the inexorably approaching first night that is bound to be the last. And so on all three fronts the non-relenting human war on deadly threats is waged. And from all three sources infinite supplies of fear may be drawn for (profitable) recycling.

For that reason, many battles may be won in the perpetual war against fear – and yet the war itself seems to be anything but winnable.

2

Fear and Evil

Evil and fear are Siamese twins. You can't meet one without meeting the other. Or perhaps they are but two names of one experience – one of the names referring to what you see or what you hear, the other to what you feel; one pointing 'out there', to the world, the other to the 'in here', to yourself. What we fear, is evil; what is evil, we fear.

But what is evil? This is an incurably flawed question, even though so stubbornly and untiringly asked: we are doomed to search in vain for an answer from the moment we have asked it. The question 'what is evil?' is *un*answerable because what we tend to call 'evil' is precisely the kind of wrong which we can neither understand nor even clearly articulate, let alone explain its presence to our full satisfaction. We call that kind of wrong 'evil' for the very reason that it is unintelligible, ineffable and inexplicable. 'Evil' is what defies and explodes that intelligibility which makes the world liveable . . . We can tell what 'crime' is because we have a code of laws which criminal acts breach. We know what 'sin' is because we have a list of commandments whose breach makes the perpetrators sinners. We resort to the idea of 'evil' when we cannot point to what rule has been broken or bypassed for the occurrence of the act for which we seek a proper name. All the frames we possess and use to inscribe and plot horrifying stories in order to make them comprehensible (and thereby defused and detoxified, domesticated and tamed – 'liveable with') crumble and

fall apart when we try to stretch them wide enough to accommodate the sort of wrongdoing we call 'evil', because of our inability
to spell out the set of rules such wrongdoing has breached.

This is why so many philosophers abandon all attempts to
explain the presence of evil as hopeless projects – and settle for a
statement of fact, a 'brute fact' so to speak, a fact neither calling
for, nor admitting of further explanation: evil *is*. Without saying
it in so many words, they relegate evil to the murky space of Kant's
noumena – not just unknown, but *unknowable*; a space that
eludes examination and resists discursive articulation. Cast at a
safe distance from the realm of the comprehensible, evil tends to
be invoked when we insist on explaining the inexplicable. We
cling to it as to a last resort in our desperate search for an *explan-
ans* (that which explains); but moving it to the position of an
explanandum (the object of explanation) would require stepp-
ing beyond the reach of human reason. We can only settle for
Candide's advice and *cultiver notre jardin* (tend our garden) – and
focus on *phenomena*, on things our senses may perceive and our
reason may conceive, while leaving the *noumenal* where it belongs
(that is, beyond the limits of human comprehension) and from
where it refuses to come out and from where we are impotent to
draw it out.

Reason is a permanent and universal attribute of human beings
– but what it can embrace and what it can't depends on its toolbox
and routines; and both tend to change over time. Both grow in
size and effectiveness; and yet, bafflingly and infuriatingly, the
more powerful they seem to grow, the more impotent reason's
tools become when it comes to thrusting evil into the order of the
intelligible; while the more efficient the routines are, the less fit
they are to tackle that task.

For the larger part of Europe's history the idea of evil's incurable incomprehensibility would hardly have come up. For our
ancestors, evil was born or awakened in the act of sinning and
returned to sinners in the shape of punishment. Were humans to
follow Divine commandments unflinchingly and routinely choose
goodness over evil, evil would have nowhere to come from. Whatever evil there was in the universe could be traced back whole,
with no residue, to human beings – their wrong deeds and sinful
thoughts. The presence of evil – any kind of evil, floods and
plagues affecting everyone as much as individually suffered mis-

fortunes – was a *moral* problem, and fighting evil back and forcing it to disappear was a *moral* task. With sin and punishment as the principal thinking tools in the toolbox of reason, contrition and atonement were the natural and trustworthy routines to deploy in the search for immunity from evil and in the fight to evict evil from the world of humans.

Just as psychoanalysts, taking it on Freud's authority that all psychical afflictions have their roots in harrowing childhood experiences, would carry on unearthing the childhood sources of adult complexes, experiences they believe their patients *must* have had but later must have suppressed and forgotten, and just as they would not admit the futility of their search however tiresome and stubbornly ineffective their search might so far have been (while their patients carry on keeping their appointments, however long their thus-far unsuccessful therapy might have dragged on), the sages of those other, more ancient times, who knew that all evil was a deserved and equitably apportioned punishment for the sins committed by the sufferers, would carry on pressing the faithful to confess and admit the sins which they believed the sufferers *must have* committed but were afterwards denying and refusing to admit. No string of ineffective pressures and unrewarded efforts to pinpoint the sin-behind-the-evil, however long, would be long enough to reach the conclusion that the belief which made sense of the tools and routines deployed was ill-conceived or downright false, or even that the link between sin (the cause) and evil (the effect) was somewhat less unexceptional than that belief implied. To hedge bets and firm up the belief just in case it might be shaken, the doctrine of evil-as-punishment-for-sins was supplemented by codicils designed to counter in advance any evidence to the contrary: codicils like St Augustine's doctrine of the species-wide hereditariness of original sin, or Calvin's teaching that the allocation of Divine grace and damnation preceded human efforts at salvation and was then irreversible, non-negotiable and immune to whatever individual humans might later do.

All such axioms might have been sufficient for popular consumption; they wouldn't however suffice for the sages themselves. For many centuries, the Book of Job, which threw open the mysteries of evil that the simple sequence of sin and punishments tried to cover up instead of resolving them, remained a sharp thorn in philosophy's and theology's flesh. That Book condensed and articulated the otherwise diffuse and ineffable experience of 'undeserved evil' (and obliquely of 'unearned grace'), as well as sketching and rehearsing in advance virtually all the arguments that would be advanced through centuries by successive generations of theologians to save (or much less often to refute) the doctrine of the immoral, and nothing but immoral, roots of evil and the moral, and nothing but moral, nature of the means to repulse evil or prevent it happening.

The story told in the Book of Job was the most insidious of challenges to the assumed order of things and the least easy to repel. Given the contents of the toolbox and the routines currently available to reason, the story of Job was a gauntlet thrown down to the very possibility of making the creatures endowed with reason, and therefore yearning for logic, feel at home in the world. Just like the ancient astronomers who desperately drew ever new epicycles to defend the geocentric world-order against the unruly evidence of night-sky sightings, the learned theologians quoted in the Book of Job leaned over backwards to defend the unbreakability of the sin-and-punishment and virtue-and-reward links against the evidence steadily supplied of pains inflicted on a God-fearing, pious creature, a true paragon of virtue. As if their resounding failure to advance convincing arguments (not to mention clinching proofs) that the credibility of routine explanations of evil had emerged unscathed from the acid test of pious Job's misfortune was not yet enough to dash all prospects of comprehension, the dense fog in which the allocation of good and bad luck was tightly shrouded did not disperse when God himself joined the debate . . .

Job's begging, 'Tell me plainly, and I will listen in silence: show me where I have erred . . . Why hast thou made me thy butt, and why have I become thy target?' (Job 6: 24; 7: 20), waited in vain for God's answer. Job expected that much: 'Indeed this I know for the truth, that no man can win his case against God. If a man chooses to argue with him, God will not answer one question in a thousand . . . Though I am right, I get no answer . . . Blameless, I say . . . But it is all one; therefore I say: He destroys blameless and wicked alike' (Job 9: 2–3; 9: 15, 22).

Job expected no answer to his complaint, and at least on this point he was evidently in the right. God ignored his question, and questioned instead Job's right to ask: 'Brace yourself and stand like a man; I will ask questions, and you shall answer. Dare you deny that I am just or put me in the wrong that you may be right? Have you an arm like God's arm, can you thunder with a voice like his?' (Job 40: 6–9). God's questions were only rhetorical, of course; Job knew all too well that he had no arm or voice to match God's, and so by implication he was aware that it was not God who owed him explanations but it was he who owed God an apology (let's note that according to the Book it was God's questions, not Job's, that came 'out of the tempest' – that archetype of all other blows known to be deaf to all immolation and to strike at random . . .).

What Job might have been as yet unaware of was that all the earthly pretenders to God-like omnipotence in the centuries to come would find the unpredictability and haphazardness of their thunder to be by far the most awesome, most terrorizing and invincible of their weapons; and that whoever might wish to steal the ruler's thunder must first disperse the fog of uncertainty that shrouds it and recast randomness into regularity. But then Job could not anticipate that; he was not a creature of modernity.

Susan Neiman[1] and Jean-Pierre Dupuy[2] have recently suggested that the quick succession of earthquake, fire and high tide that jointly destroyed Lisbon in 1755 marked the beginning of the modern philosophy of evil. Modern philosophers set *natural* disasters apart from *moral* evils – the difference being precisely the *randomness* of the first (now recast as blindness) and *intentionality* or *purposefulness* of the second.

Neiman points out that 'since Lisbon, natural evils no longer have any seemly relations to moral evils, since they no longer have meaning at all' (Husserl suggested that *Meinung*, 'meaning', comes from *meinen*, 'intending'; later, post-Husserl, generations of philosophers would take it for granted that there is no meaning without intention). Lisbon was like a stage production of the story of Job, performed on the Atlantic coast in full glare of publicity and all Europe's view – though this time God was to be largely absent from the dispute that followed the event.

True to the nature of all disputes, standpoints differed. According to Dupuy, it was paradoxically Jean-Jacques Rousseau, who due to his celebration of the pristine wisdom of everything 'natural' was all too often mistaken for a hopelessly pre- and anti-modern thinker, who struck the most modern chord. In his open letter to Voltaire, Rousseau insisted that if not the Lisbon disaster itself, then most certainly its catastrophic consequences and their hor-rifying scale resulted from human, not nature's, faults (note: *faults*, not *sins* – unlike God, nature had no faculties to judge the moral quality of human deeds): the products of human myopia, not nature's blindness; and of human mundane greed, not nature's lofty indifference. If only 'the residents of that large city had dis-persed more evenly, and built lighter houses, the damage would have been much smaller, perhaps even none at all . . . And how many wretches lost their lives in the catastrophe because they wished to collect their belongings – some their papers, some others their money?'[3]

In the long run at least, Rousseau-style arguments came out on top. Modern philosophy followed the pattern set by Pombal, the Prime Minister of Portugal at the time of the Lisbon catastrophe, whose concerns and actions 'focused on eradicating those evils that could be reached by human hands'.[4] And let's add that modern philosophers expected/hoped/believed that human hands, once they had been equipped with scientifically designed and techno-logically supplied extensions, would stretch out longer. They also trusted that as human hands lengthened, the number of evils remaining outside their reach would fall; even to zero, given enough time and sufficient resolve.

Two and a half centuries later we can however opine that what the philosophical and non-philosophical pioneers of modernity expected to happen was not to be. As Neiman sums up the lessons of the two centuries separating Lisbon, which triggered modern ambitions, from Auschwitz, which collapsed them,

> Lisbon revealed how remote the world is from humans; Auschwitz revealed the remoteness of humans from themselves. If disentan-gling the natural from the human is part of the modern project, the distance between Lisbon and Auschwitz showed how difficult it was to keep them apart . . .
> If Lisbon marked the moment of recognition that traditional theodicy was hopeless, Auschwitz signaled the recognition that every replacement fared no better.[5]

The modern cognitive frame fared no better either in the effort of cracking the mystery of evil than did the frames which enabled/

constrained the efforts of the Book-of-Job theologians – the frames which the modern mind emphatically rejected and had hoped to put paid to forever.

Hannah Arendt explains the shock and bewilderment most of us felt when we first heard of Auschwitz, and the gesture of despair with which we responded to the news, by the excruciating difficulty of the task of absorbing its truth and accommodating it in the picture of the world we think with and live through; a picture based on 'the assumption current in all modern legal systems that intent to do wrong is necessary for the commission of a crime'.[6]

That assumption was indeed an invisible presence on the defendant's bench throughout Eichmann's Jerusalem trial. With the help of his learned lawyers, Eichmann tried to convince the court that since his only motive was the *job well done* (that is, *done to the satisfaction of his superiors*), his motives bore no relation to the nature and fate of the objects of his actions; that whether Eichmann-the-person did or did not harbour a grudge against Jews was neither here nor there (he and his lawyers swore that he harboured no grudge, and certainly no hatred – even if by their own criteria that circumstance was also irrelevant), and that personally he could not stomach the sight of murder, let alone mass murder. In other words, Eichmann and his lawyers implied that the death of about six million humans was but a side-effect (one is tempted to deploy the 'new and improved', post-Iraq vocabulary and say 'collateral damage') of a motivation to loyal service (that is, of a virtue most painstakingly and lovingly groomed in all functionaries of modern bureaucracies – while ostensibly harking back to the 'workmanship instinct', a yet older, genuinely venerable and even more sacrosanct human quality, the virtue cast at the very centre of modern work ethics). 'Intent to do wrong' was, therefore, absent – so Eichmann and his lawyers argued – as there was nothing wrong in the fulfilment of one's duty to the best possible effect, according to someone else's intention, higher up in the hierarchy. What would be 'wrong', on the contrary, was an intention to disobey the orders.

What can be gleaned from Eichmann's defence (destined to be repeated, in countless variants, by countless perpetrators of countless characteristically modern acts of 'categorial murder') is that hatred and the desire to make the victim disappear from the world are not necessary conditions of murder – and that if some people suffer as a result of some other people's fulfilment of their duties, a charge of *immorality* therefore does not apply. Making the victims suffer is even less a *crime* in the understanding of modern law, which insists that unless a motive for murder has been found the culprit ought to be classified not as a criminal but a sick person, a psychopath or sociopath, and needs to be committed for psychiatric treatment, rather than to prison or the gallows. And let's add that such an understanding is still, many years after Eichmann's trial, shared by most people socialized into modern settings. It is reinforced, and by the sheer frequency of reinforcements corroborated, through being daily restated in Hollywood-produced whodunnits and police soaps on millions of screens around the modern world.

In modern practice, unlike in the modern replacement of the orthodox theodicy, which fared no better than the theodicy it was meant to replace, men and women could however be expected (and so could be feared) to do evil *without* evil intention. Ordinary men and women. Just like you and me. Motives for action were irrelevant – perhaps even an unnecessary luxury better to be avoided because of the exorbitant costs of their inculcation and cultivation. But a yet more important reason not to rely on the executors' motives was the threat that if the task is given hostage to specific intentions and convictions it may go awry in the event that the motivation, not cultivated vigorously enough, runs dry, or if it is quashed by another motive because it wasn't being staunchly enough promoted. Just think: were the unswerving obedience of workers to the rhythm of the assembly line to depend on their love of the automobile, or worse still on their adoration of a particular brand or mark of the vehicle, what chance would the car industry have had to meet its production targets, what certainty that the line would go on running smoothly as long as it was needed? Emotions are fidgety and flickery, they quickly run out of steam, they tend to be drawn away from the target by a slightest distraction. To put it briefly, they are untrustworthy and unreliable. And as Sabini and Silver mused when considering the logic of genocide – alongside the car production, another mass industry of the modern era:

> Emotions, and their biological basis, have a natural time course; lust, even blood lust, is eventually sated. Further, emotions are

notoriously fickle, can be turned. A lynch mob is unreliable, it can sometimes be moved by sympathy – say by a child's suffering. To eradicate a 'race' it is essential to kill the children . . . Thorough, comprehensive, exhaustive murder required the replacement of the mob with bureaucracy, the replacement of shared rage with obedience to authority. The requisite bureaucracy would be effective whether manned by extreme or tepid anti-Semites, considerably broadening the pool of potential recruits . . .[7]

Hannah Arendt spied out the banality of modern evil in Eichmann's *thoughtlessness*. But inability to think or avoidance of thinking was the last misdemeanour of which Eichmann could stand accused. He was a fully fledged bureaucrat, as if descended straight from Max Weber's clean and pristine ideal type untarnished by any earthly impurities that tend to muddle the clarity of purpose-focused reason. Good bureaucrats worth their salt *must be thoughtful*. They, as we know from Max Weber, must stretch their intelligence and powers of judgement to the limit. They must carefully select the most adequate means to the end they have been told to attain. They need to deploy reason to select the shortest, cheapest and least risky way to the appointed destination. They need to set apart objects and moves relevant to the task from irrelevant ones, and select the moves that bring the target closer while pushing out of the way everything that makes the target more difficult to hit. They need to scan the matrix of possibilities and choose the most felicitous (read: most effective) permutations. They need to measure and to calculate. They need, in fact, to be supreme masters of rational calculus.

Modern bureaucrats must, in other words, excel in all the skills justly praised for their key role in securing all the mind-boggling achievements for which modern reason is rightly lauded and of which we, its possessors/employers/beneficiaries, are (also rightly) so proud. What they must not do is allow themselves to be diverted from the straight path of sober, and uncompromisingly task-focused, rationality; not by compassion, pity, shame, conscience, sympathy or antipathy to the 'objects', nor by loyalties or commitments other than commitment to the task and loyalty to all the fellow bureaucrats committed as they are to its performance and to subordinates hoping to be sheltered from their responsibility for the consequences of their own committed labour.

Emotions are many and speak in different, often discordant, voices; reason is one and has only one voice. The distinction of evil bureaucratically administered and performed is not so much its *banality* (particularly if set and seen against the evils that used to haunt societies before modern bureaucracy and its 'scientific management of labour' had been invented) as its *rationality*.

Viewed retrospectively, the modern wager on human reason (which the incalculabity of nature, made blatantly and shockingly evident by the Lisbon disaster, inspired or at least rendered as imperative as all 'last resort' measures tend to be) looks more like the starting point of a long detour. At the end of that detour, we seem to have come back to where we started from: to the horrors of incalculable, unpredictable evil, striking at random. Though wiser after the long journey than our ancestors were at its beginning, we are no longer confident that the road away from the nature-like catastrophes can be found. 'Contemporary probabilities threaten even early modern attempts to divide moral from natural evils,' observes Susan Neiman.[8] At the end of a long voyage of (unintended) discovery undertaken in the hope that it would place humanity at a safe distance from cruel, since unfeeling and callous, nature, humanity found itself facing human-made evils every bit as cruel, unfeeling, callous, random and impossible to anticipate (let alone to nip in the bud) as were the Lisbon earthquake, fire and high tide.

Evils *made by humans* appear now as unexpected as their *natural* predecessors/companions/successors. As Juan Goytisolo suggested in his *Landscapes after the Battle*, they come to be known and understandable, if at all, only when 'looking back and analysing things in retrospect'; before that, they gather force imperceptibly, infiltrating 'gradually, in silence, in seemingly harmless stages . . . like an underground stream that swells and broadens before suddenly and impetuously surfacing' – just as natural catastrophes, which the modern spirit swore to conquer, did, do, and in all probability will.

There seems to be no defence against that invisible swelling and broadening if moral scruples, pangs of conscience, impulses of human compassion and aversion to inflicting pain on humans are eroded, left to drown and swept a way. To quote Hannah Arendt again, 'Since the whole of respectable society had in one way or another succumbed to Hitler, the moral maxims which determine human behaviour and the religious commandments – *'Thou shalt not kill'* – which guide conscience had virtually vanished.'[9] We know now that 'whole societies' may succumb, 'in one way or another', to Hitlers, and we know as well that we will learn that they have succumbed only if we live long enough to find out; if, in other words, we survive their surrender. We won't notice 'the swelling and broadening of the stream' just as we did not notice the swelling of Tsunami tides – because we have been successfully trained to avert our eyes and plug our ears. Or perhaps we have been taught that 'things like this' do not happen in our comfortable and gentle, civilized and rational modern society. And yet, as Hans Mommsen reminds us:

> While Western Civilization has developed the means for unimaginable mass-destruction, the training provided by modern technology and techniques of rationalization has produced a purely technocratic and bureaucratic mentality . . . To this extent the history of the Holocaust seems to be the *mene tekel* of the modern state.[10]

His hope/conviction that humans may do a better job of the battle against evil than inanimate nature did was invested by Immanuel Kant in human, all too human and only human reason. It is reason, he pointed out, that tells us to 'act only according to that maxim by which you can at the same time will that it would become a universal law'. What we have however discovered since Kant wrote down that most famous rendition of the categorical imperative is that the road along which reason guided us through modern centuries led nowhere near the *universalization* of the maxims which we – all of us in our own and separate ways – struggled to make applicable to *us*. In that struggle, the universal *application* (if not universal *applicability*) of maxims (and so of the criteria by which people's deeds are deemed fit to be judged) proved to be the least of our, and other people's, concerns. In competition with Kant's commandment of universality, another maxim – *deux poids, deux mesures* ('two weights, two measures') – appeared to be a safe bet. In stark distinction from the implications of Kant's categorical imperative, this 'really victorious' maxim relates to a 'universal law' like chalk to cheese.

As it happens, modern reason proved to be especially apt and keen in shaping *monopolies* and founding *exclusivity* of rights. It proved to be reaching full satisfaction at the moment when the *privilege* of having a desirable rule applied had been assured *for those who acted in its name*; if, for the purpose of making that privilege secure, the application of the self-same maxim had to be or was seen as having to be refused *to some other specimens of humanity* (because of their assumed ineptitude, unworthiness, or any other reason deemed convenient but declared obvious, imperative and beyond discussion) modern reason did not seem to mind or be eager to raise objections, except in (some) securely isolated and notoriously sound-insulated offices of academic philosophers. Reason did not protest either when outside and sometimes inside those offices declarations were heard that the suffering of some people was a good price to pay for the alleviation of discomforts that might harrow some others – that is, if 'we' were the ones who happened to be those 'others' whose discomforts were to be alleviated, even though it was *our* reason that could/should have objected to the price. Just imagine that Hitler had managed to drop a couple of atomic bombs on Britain or America before he lost the war and before his henchmen were brought to court, wouldn't we have added that accomplishment to the list of Nazi crimes against humanity? And would we not have brought the commanders of Guantanamo and Baghram camps to court if they had acted on behalf of Castro's Cuba, Milosevic's Serbia or Saddam's Iraq?

In blatant opposition to the strategy implied by Kant's categorical imperative, modern rationality progressed towards freedom, security or happiness undisturbed by worry about the extent to which, if at all, the forms of happiness, security or happiness it devised were fit to become universal human possessions. Thus far, modern reason served *privilege*, not *universality*, and the desire for superiority and for secure foundations for superiority – not the dream of universality – was its driving force and the cause of its most spectacular achievements.

Before Auschwitz (or the Soviet Gulag, or Hiroshima . . .) we did not know just how awesome and horrifying the variety of evil made by humans, moral-evil-turning-natural, could become once it was able to avail itself of the new tools and weapons supplied by modern science and technology. What we did not know either at that now distant and difficult to imagine 'before' (and still admit only reluctantly, or refuse altogether to admit, in spite of the knowledge being available now in profusion) is that the logic of modern life radically, and on an unheard-of scale, expands the catchment area for the recruitment of potential evil-doers. The most terrifying lesson of Auschwitz, the Gulag, Hiroshima is that contrary to the view commonly held, though each time held in a partisan way, it is not only monsters who commit monstrous crimes; and that if it were only monsters who did, the most monstrous and terrifying of crimes we know of would not have happened. They would not even be plotted for the lack of adequate equipment, and most certainly would fail to be seen through for the lack of adequate 'human resources'.

The most morally devastating lesson of Auschwitz or the Gulag or Hiroshima is not that we could be put behind barbed wire or herded into gas chambers, but that (under the right conditions) we could stand on guard and sprinkle white crystals into chimney ducts; and not that an atomic bomb can be dropped on *our* heads, but that (under the right conditions) *we* could drop it on other people's heads. A yet greater horror, truly a meta-horror, an incubator in which all other horrors gestate, derives from the realization that when I write these words or when you read them, we both, deep in our hearts, desire such thoughts to vanish, and when they refuse to go away we allow evils to 'swell and broaden', secure in their invisibility – by leaning over backwards to refute them, questioning their credibility, and dismissing them as merely crying wolf, while remaining oblivious to our duty to recall and ponder what Hannah Arendt found in the reports submitted by the learned psychologists called to testify in Eichmann's trial:

> Half a dozen psychiatrists had certified him as 'normal' – 'More normal, at any rate, than I am after examining him', one of them was said to have exclaimed, while another found that his whole psychological outlook, his attitude towards his wife and children, mother and father, brothers, sisters and friends, was 'not only normal but most desirable' – and finally the minister who had paid regular visits to him in prison after the Supreme Court had finished hearing the appeal reassured everybody by declaring Eichmann to be 'a man with very positive ideas'.[11]

Eichmann's victims were 'people like us'. But so were – perish the thought – many of Eichmann's executors, their slaughterers; and Eichmann? Both thoughts ooze fear. But while the first thought is a call to action, the second disables and incapacitates, whispering that resistance to evil is in vain. This is perhaps why we resist that second thought so strongly. One fear that is genuinely and hopelessly unbearable is the fear of the invincibility of evil.

And yet, as Primo Levi put it in his book-long last will and testament: there is no doubt, every one of us can, potentially, become a monster.[12] It would be better for all of us – more soothing, more comfortable, though alas not safer – to believe that evil is just the (D)evil hiding under a shortened name, clipped by a single letter (like the criminal on a 'wanted' list who, to escape capture, shaves his beard or moustache). The terrible news, however, is that Eichmann was not the Devil. He was an unexeptional, dull, boringly 'ordinary' creature: someone you pass by on a street without noticing. As a husband, father or neighbour he would hardly stand out from the crowd. He was the average, the median, the mean of demographic statistical tables – as he would surely be of psychological statistical tables, and of *moral* ones (were we able to compute them). He just, as we all do, preferred his own comfort to that of others. It is that common, *ordinary* malfeasance or lapse that at an *extra*ordinary time leads to *extra*ordinary results. Once we know that, we don't need the Devil any longer. Worse still, we are now unable to take the 'Devil hypothesis' seriously when (if) it is offered. And worst of all, the Devil of that hypothesis would perhaps seem to us laughably inept and clumsy when compared to that trivially reasonable fellow on the defendant's bench in the Jerusalem courtroom.

The most seminal, and arguably the most sinister consequence of that discovery is the present-day crisis of trust. Trust is in trouble the moment we know that evil may hide *anywhere*; that it does not stand out from the crowd, does not bear distinctive marks and carries no identity card; and that *everyone* may be found to be currently in its service, to be its reservist on temporary leave or its potential conscript.

Of course, such a view is a gross exaggeration; surely not *everyone* is fit and willing to be evil's servant. Surely, there are uncountable numbers of people sufficiently immune and averse to evil to withstand its blandishments or threats – and wide-eyed enough to recognize them as of evil's making. The point is, though, that you won't know who they are and how to tell them from those who are more vulnerable to evil's schemings. Would you recognize a mass murderer in Eichmann if you met him only as a neighbour on the staircase of your appartment block or, say, a fellow member of the parents' school council or of a local camera club? If you think that you would, ask the Serbs, Croats and Muslims of Bosnia who spent most of their lives drinking wine and slivovitz in each other's company while blissfully unaware of what temple, if any, and on what days of the week, if any, their companions, next-door neighbours and workmates attended – until the day, that is, when without much warning the 'conditions' became 'right' to find out, and to find out in the hardest and most terrifying of all possible ways. And if this is how things are and may yet turn out to be, if there is no telling how resistant to evil the people around you will prove and be found to be the moment when 'conditions become right', what practical benefit can you derive from being (correctly) aware that not all people are equally likely to fall prey to evil? For all practical purposes, the odds against your safety stay unchanged, whatever opinion you hold of the moral qualities of the human beings around you. You are bound to grapple in the dark. You can only guess (and guesses are notoriously risky) who will, and who will not succumb to the temptation of evil at the moment of test. So (as experts on risk calculation will tell you) the assumption that all people without exception are prone to be recruited into the service of evil looks like the safest bet. Keep your eyes wide open, never allow your vigilance to lapse. In other words, as the subtitle of an American Reality TV series says in an alert to its millions of avid viewers, grateful for the 'enlightenment' they have been offered: *trust nobody*.

Most of the time, except for brief carnivals of 'targeted solidarity' in response to particularly horrifying disasters, 'targeted mournings' caused by the sudden death of an idol, or equally brief though particularly explosive and rowdy outbursts of 'targeted patriotism' during world cups, cricket tournaments and similar occasions for focused emotional release, the 'others' (others as *strangers*, anonymous, faceless others met daily in passing, or milling around the densely populated cities) are sources of a vague, diffuse threat rather than giving a feeling of security and insurance against danger. No solidarity is expected from them and none is aroused by seeing them – and there is even a fear of routinely breaching the thin protective veneer of Erving Goffman's 'civil inattention'. Keeping your distance seems the only reasonable way to proceed. As Eduardo Mendietta observes, 'cities which historically and conceptually used to be the metonym of security and safety have turned into sources of threat and violence.'[13] The various specimens of 'bunker architecture', as the preferred choice of city residence for those who can afford it, are monuments to the suspected threats and embodiments of fear that cities arouse. The 'modern architectural bunker'

> has no visible entry and no balconies or terraces. These buildings do not open out onto the street, nor face the public square, nor monumentalize the political and economic power of a city. Instead, these buildings are linked to other similar buildings by covered bridges suspended over the streets, while they face away from the centre of the city, and more often than not are sheathed in a dark glass that reflects the sky, mountains and landscape rather than the face of the city itself. Their monumentality gestures contempt for the urban . . .

For human bonds, the crisis of trust is bad news. From well-protected and secluded clearings, places where one had hoped to take off (at last!) the heavy armour and stiff mask having to be worn in the harsh, competitive world out there, in the wilderness, the 'networks' of human bonds turn into frontier territories where interminable reconnaissance skirmishes need to be engaged in day in, day out. If trust is missing and credits of confidence are offered and expected to be offered only reluctantly, if at all, yesterday's armistice terms do not seem a safe ground on which to rest a secure prognosis for tomorrow's peace. With the norms regulating mutual duties and obligations thrown into a melting pot, and none boasting a comfortably lengthy life expectancy, there are few if any constants in the equations which one struggles daily to solve; making calculations feels more like tackling a puzzle with only a few scattered, ambiguous and unreliable clues. All in all, human relations are no longer sites of certainty, tranquillity and spiritual comfort. They become instead a prolific source of anxiety. Instead of offering the coveted rest, they promise perpetual anxiety and a life on the alert. Distress signals will never stop flashing, tocsins will never stop sounding.

That in our liquid modern times we need and desire firm and reliable bonds more than at any other time only exacerbates the anxiety. While unable to put our suspicions to rest and stop sniffing out treachery and fearing frustration, we seek – compulsively and passionately – wider 'networks' of friends and friendship; indeed, as wide a 'network' as we can manage to squeeze into the mobile phone directory that, obligingly, grows more capacious with every new generation of mobiles. And as we try to hedge our bets against treachery and reduce our risks in this way, we incur more risks and set the stage for more betrayals. Since no one basket is totally foolproof, we try to put eggs in as many as we can find.

We prefer to vest our hopes in 'networks' rather than partnerships, hoping that in a network there will always be some mobile phone numbers available for sending and receiving messages of loyalty. We hope to compensate for the lack of quality with quantity (the probability of winning in a lottery is minuscule; but perhaps several miserable probabilities will amount to one a bit more decent?). Spread the risks, hedge your bets – this seems to be the most prudent way to go. The tracks left behind by such a pursuit of safety look however like a graveyard of dashed hopes and frustrated expectations, and the way ahead is strewn with shallow and fragile relationships. The ground does not get firmer with successive steps; if anything, it feels still more slushy and unfit for settling down on. It prompts walkers to run, and runners to run even faster.

Partnerships do not grow stronger, fears do not dissipate. Neither does the suspicion of an evil patiently waiting its chance. In haste, there is no time to find out just how far the suspicion is warranted – let alone to stop the evil emerging from its hiding place. The denizens of the liquid modern world seasoned in practising the art of liquid modern life tend to regard running away from trouble as a better bet than fighting it. At the first sign of evil they look for a getaway route with a reliably heavy door to lock behind them. The line dividing friends for life and enemies forever, once so clearly drawn and closely watched, is all but washed away; it peters out in a sort of 'grey zone' in which assigned roles may be exchanged instantly and with little effort.

The boundary, or whatever is left of it, changes shape and moves with every step – and in the life of a runner there are many steps still expected to be taken. All that adds to the already considerable confusion and shrouds the future in a yet denser mist. And mist – inscrutable, opaque, impermeable – is (as even a little child will tell you) a favourite hiding place of Evil. Made of the vapours of fear, mist reeks of evil.

3

Horror of the Unmanageable

Humanity, as Jean-Pierre Dupuy points out in his most recent studies,[1] has, in the course of the last century, reached the capacity of self-destruction. What threatens the planet now is not just another round of self-inflicted damage (a rather constant feature of human history), and not another of the long string of catastrophes (which have befallen humanity time and again on the road to its present condition), but a catastrophe to end all catastrophes, a catastrophe that would leave no human being behind to record it, ponder it and derive a lesson from it, let alone to learn and apply that lesson.

Humanity now has all the weapons needed to commit collective suicide, whether by design or default – to annihilate itself while taking the rest of life on the planet to perdition. Its self-appointed or elected plenipotentiaries even came to the conclusion at some point that a realistic prospect of its self-demise is a necessary condition and the best chance of its survival: that keeping the threat of mutual (and in fact self-) annihilation alive (that is, inventing, producing and stockpiling the ever more refined tools of organized mass murder necessary to give credence to MAD – Mutually Assured Destruction) is indeed indispensable to the postponement of its extinction. The 'theory' of MAD has fallen somewhat out of fashion now, having caused enough outcry to be, even if reluctantly, declared politically incorrect – and it is seldom preached in public in an explicit, uncamouflaged form;

but the strategy born of and inspired by the MAD doctrine is still very much a going concern, followed faithfully by those already able to follow it, and acting as an inspiration and dream-target for those who, as yet, can't.

Warehouses full to bursting with nuclear warheads, and missiles ready to deliver them to every nook and cranny of the planet, are just one of the ultimate catastrophes waiting to happen. Looming self-destruction may arrive in many other avatars; the explosion of weapons explicitly targeted at destroying life is one of many. Yet more sinister, since it is an unintended variant of self-destruction, taking shape and advancing surreptitiously and in a roundabout way ('swelling and broadening invisibly', as Juan Goytisolo would have said), is the prospect of making the planet unliveable for humans, and perhaps for any other known form of life. What makes this kind of ultimate catastrophe particularly perfidious and its advance particularly difficult to monitor, let alone to stave off, is that its imminence is, paradoxically, the direct though seldom pondered and hardly ever planned outcome of human efforts to make the planet *more* hospitable and *more* comfortable for humans to live in.

The forms taken by such efforts have been made to the measure, as it were, of the selected populations – designed and practised, even if not explicitly declared, as a local privilege. Though some lip-service was paid, no serious consideration was given to the plausibility of applying them universally, species-wide; most certainly, no practical conclusions were drawn from such consideration. No wonder the resulting comforts were unevenly distributed from the start, and the areas where they condensed remain to this day relatively few and far between. As Jacques Attali observed in *La Voie humaine*, half of world trade and more than half of global investment benefit just twenty-two countries accommodating a mere 14 per cent of the world's population, whereas the forty-nine poorest countries inhabited by 11 per cent of the world's population receive between them just a half of 1 per cent share of the global product – just about the same as the combined income of the three wealthiest men on the planet. Let me add that Tanzania, for instance, one of those poorer countries, earns 2.2 billion dollars a year which it divides among 25 million inhabitants, whereas Goldman Sachs banking firm earns 2.6 billion dollars, which is then divided between 161 stockholders. To complete the picture: at the time I am writing these words, there are no break-waters in sight capable of stemming the global tide of income polarization.

Deepening inequality is not an accidental, neglected but in principle rectifiable side-effect of certain uncalled-for, recklessly embarked on and insufficiently monitored undertakings, nor a result of a regrettable but rectifiable malfunctioning of an essentially sound system. It is rather an integral part of a conception of human happiness and comfortable living, and of the strategy which that conception dictates; the conception and strategy can be contemplated and entertained *only as privileges*, and are blatantly unsuitable for stretching wider – let alone for being stretched widely enough to be shared by the whole of humankind. To be so stretched, they would require the resources of at least three planets, not one. There are just not enough resources on earth to sustain the bids of China, India and Brazil (not to mention similar bids that may shortly be made by populations currently falling behind) to copy or imitate the forms in which the comforts of life have been thus far pursued and are presently enjoyed in the US, Canada, Western Europe or Australia, the places where these life motives and stimuli were first shaped, and are still being shaped and put ever more keenly into operation.

The 'universalizability' of newly invented forms of life, deemed more comfortable, was never a criterion guiding their adoption and cultivation. Modern developments in such selected enclaves of the planet as mustered enough power to seek and find gratifications for their *locally* gestated ambitions in *global* space, and to mobilize *global* resources to sustain their *local* enjoyments, were guided by a logic which – in blatant violation of the modernizers' proclaimed intentions – made the species-wide spread of such ambitions a truly catastrophic prospect, and so for all practical intents and purposes *precluded the possibility of their own universalization*.

Modern developments could not have occurred and most certainly would not have been able to proceed at the pace they acquired if the issue of their 'natural' and unencroachable spatial limits had not been argued away and actively repressed, or simply removed from view by being struck off the list of factors included in the instrumental-rational calculations. They would not have begun, and if they had they would have promptly ground to a halt, had the limits of the planet's endurability been recognized and admitted, seriously considered and respected, and if more than occasional and perfunctory lip-service had been paid to the precept of universality and human equality. If, in short, the pro-moters and practitioners of the modern concept of development had felt obliged to refrain from the excess and wastefulness which the 'really deployed' strategy of progressive improvement neces-sarily entailed.

Drawing inspiration from the analyses of the late Ivan Illich, Dupuy tracks the inherently wasteful nature and the ultimately self-destructive tendency of modern developments down to the strategy of 'detours'; a tendency bound to render the objectives of the strategy ever more distant and, whether by design or default, to cast them sooner or later beyond reach.

The strategy of detours consists of substituting a long chain of heteronomous events, mostly performed by artefacts, for the much shorter action-loops autonomously undertaken by humans. According to the calculations of Dupuy and his associates, if the distance actually covered by the average owner of a car was divided, as it ought to be, by the number of hours she or he puts in to drive it, service it and earn the costs of its purchase, it would transpire that the combustion-engine revolution in transport, intended to radically speed up human spatial movements, has enabled a movement of about four miles per hour – roughly the walking speed of an ordinary pedestrian and much less than the velocity easily reached by a bicyclist. Illich himself famously exposed a similar 'detour' (in that case the replacement of a healthy lifestyle by a steadily lengthening chain of medical/phar-maceutical interventions) as the principal moving force of modern medicine.[2] In addition, Illich's study brought into particularly sharp relief the endemic tendency of all detours to expand them-selves and render their own completion all but impossible: as he found out, an ever growing proportion of medical practices were caused by the need to repair or make up for the unanticipated or played-down adverse effects of previously applied 'detours'.

It needs to be repeated again and again that the impending 'ultimate catastrophe' is being brought nearer by the inner logic of modern life. The prospect of catastrophe is particularly difficult to avert since modern civilization owes its morbid (or rather suicidal) potential to the selfsame qualities from which it draws its grandeur and glamour: to its inborn aversion to self-limitation, its inherent transgressiveness and its resentment of, and disrespect for, all and any borders and limits – especially the idea of final, ultimate limits.

'Modernity' is conceivable only as a continuous, obsessive and compulsive modernization – that shorthand name for building ever new and ever longer detours, more often than not disguised as short cuts. It concedes only a temporary, indeed short-lived power to obstacles: it grants them at best the status of temporary constraints, tolerated for a time, but bound soon to be scrapped, bypassed or pushed out of the way by one more, or a few more efforts of science (technology's thoughtful reflection and brains trust) and technology (science's practical arm). Obstacles, including those among them which look suspiciously like limits, are 'problems', and problems, as we, the modern, know only too well, are challenges which set tasks that are, by definition, soluble.

Busy resolving successive problems, and particularly the problems brought about by the last or the last-but-one problem-solving effort, modern civilization has neither the time nor the inner urge to reflect on the darkness at the far end of the tunnel. It is prone to disasters that regularly take the current problem-fighters and the prospective problem-solvers by surprise. The way it deals with such disasters follows the rule of locking the stable door after the horse has bolted and has most probably run too far to be caught. And the restless spirit of modernization sees to it that there is a constantly growing, since self-multiplying, number of stable doors demanding to be locked.

At the stage we are now, a large part of daily 'progress' consists of repairing the direct or 'collateral' damage done by past and current efforts to speed it up. From these exercises in crisis management, the tasks ahead routinely emerge *less* manageable than before. And there is no knowing which of the eagerly added straws will finally break the camel's back: which of the successive managerial operations will make the task finally and unredeemably unmanageable.

Being modern, we are doomed to move inside the loop of problem-pinpointing-and-isolating, problem-naming and problem-solving, those specifically modern, self-propelling and self-accelerating renditions of the cycles of action and reaction, and so are unable to conceive of any alternative ways of tackling the adversities that are bound to emerge in quick succession (just as we rightly suspect the imaginary two-dimensional worm to be incapable of visualizing a move into a third dimension). We know of no medicine against the morbid effects of a detour – except another detour; no therapy for the pernicious side-effects of narrowly targeted managerial undertakings – save another narrowly targeted managerial undertaking. The issue of the limits to human enterprise has been left out of our thoughts and practices for so long that by now it has become all but incomprehensible and indeed ineffable; even the fully and truly 'natural' disasters, for which human miscalculation and mismanagement could not credibly be held responsible, we tend to transplant into the managerial discourse – as Dupuy found to be the case in the aftermath of the tsunami ('The innocence of the Asian tsunami lasted only a few days,' he observed).[3] Quoting Paul Taponnier,[4] Dupuy points out that

> the exaltation has reached its peak when it became known that the Thailand authorities were fairly quickly informed of the earthquake and the likelihood of a tsunami, but decided not to raise an alarm for the fear of damaging the country's tourist industry. The researchers were next to be named among the causes of the disaster: ignorance, insufficiency of scientific knowledge and governments that starved research of funds were appointed culprits. Moral guilt has definitively covered the ground that should have remained the domain of natural evil, on the confident assumption that the tide would have stopped at the physical obstacles there to arrest it.

Before we shrug our shoulders and smirk after reading Taponnier's report, let's consider the following.

One thing is missing in Taponnier's and Dupuy's reports. What is missing, if one failed to note it in the case of a distant (well, 'exotic') disaster like the Asian tsunami, has been brought to light by Katrina, the natural catastrophe that struck right in the heart of the most potent and resourceful of the countries at the forefront of the civilizing process.

In New Orleans and its surroundings, no one could complain that the early warning system did not work and that scientific research was starved of funds. Everybody knew that Katrina was coming, and all had quite enough time to run for shelter. Not all, though, could act on their knowledge and make good use of the time available for escape. Some – quite a few – could not scrape together enough money for flight tickets. They could pack their families in trucks – but where were they expected to take them? Motels also cost money, and money they did not have. And – paradoxically – it was easier for their well-off neighbours to obey the advice to leave their homes, abandon their property and run for their lives; their belongings were insured – Katrina might be a mortal threat to their lives, but not to their wealth. On the other hand, the possessions of those who had no money to pay for air tickets or motels, though lamentably pitiable by comparison, were their only effects; no one was going to compensate them for their loss, and once those things were lost they would be lost forever, and all their life savings with them.

Katrina may have been not choosy, may have struck the guilty and the innocent, the rich and the poor with the same cool equanimity – and yet that admittedly natural catastrophe did not feel 'natural' in the same way to all its victims. Whereas the hurricane itself was not a human product, its *consequences for humans* obviously were. As the Reverend Calvin O. Butts III, pastor of Abyssinian Baptist Church in Harlem (and he was not the only one) summed it up, 'The people affected were largely poor people. Poor, black people.'[5] As David Gonzales, *New York Times* special correspondent, put it,

> [in] the days since neighbourhoods and towns along the Gulf Coast were wiped out by the winds and water, there has been a growing sense that race and class are the unspoken markers of who got out and who got stuck. Just as in developing countries where the failures of rural development policies become glaringly clear at times of natural disasters like floods and drought, many national leaders said, some of the United States' poorest cities have been left vulnerable by federal policies.
>
> 'No one would have checked on a lot of the black people in these parishes while the sun shined,' said Mayor Milton D. Tutwiler of Winstonville, Miss. 'So am I surprised that no one has come to help us now? No.'

Martin Espada, an English professor at the University of Massachusetts, observes: 'We tend to think of natural disasters as somehow even-handed, as somehow random. Yet it has always been thus: poor people are in danger. That is what it means to be poor. It's dangerous to be poor. It's dangerous to be black. It's dangerous to be Latino.' As he implies, the categories listed as particularly exposed to danger largely overlap. Many of the poor are among the blacks and among the Latinos. Two-thirds of New Orleans residents were black and more than a quarter lived in poverty; while in the Lower Ninth Ward of the city, swept off the face of the earth by flood waters, more than 98 per cent of residents were black and more than a third lived in poverty.

No one can be sure to what extent that circumstance influenced the federal authorities when they were busy cutting the funds earmarked for the overhaul of the alarmingly inadequate anti-flood defences of the city. And no one can be sure what role the demography of the victims played in the briefing issued to the National Guard when, after unpardonably long procrastination, they were finally sent to the afflicted area, to concentrate on catching the looters and 'shooting to kill' (indiscriminately, whether thieves of electronic goods or those grasping for food and bottled water) before going on to feed the starving, shelter the homeless and bury the dead. Sending troops seems to have been prompted more by the threat to *human-made* law and order than by the urge to salvage the victims of the *natural* disaster.

The most badly injured among the victims of that natural catastrophe were the people who, well before Katrina struck, had already been the rejects of order and the refuse of modernization; victims of order-maintenance and economic progress, two eminently human enterprises.[6] Long before they found themselves at the very bottom of the list of priority concerns of the authorities responsible for the security of citizens, they had been exiled to the margins of the attention (and the political agenda) of the authorities who were declaring the pursuit of happiness to be a universal human right, and the survival of the fittest to be the prime means of implementing it.

A blood-curdling thought: did Katrina not help, inadvertently, the efforts of the ailing disposal industry of wasted humans, clearly not up to the task of coping with the social consequences of the negative globalization of a crowded (and from the waste-disposal industry's viewpoint, *over*crowded) planet? Was this helpfulness not one of the reasons why the need to despatch troops was not strongly felt until *social* order was broken and the prospect of *social* unrest came close? Which of the two 'early warning systems' ultimately signalled that need to deploy the National Guard? A thoroughly demeaning, blood-curdling thought indeed; one would dearly wish to dismiss it as unwarranted or downright fanciful, and even more be loath to articulate and record it – if only the sequence of events made it less credible than it was . . .

However strongly we resent asking such questions, events force them on our minds and consciences. As Simon Shama recently found, 'the most shocking difference between 9/11 and Katrina was in what might have been expected in the aftermath of disaster';[7] and what really did happen in that aftermath was determined by everything that had happened before the disaster – by human beings making decisions. The federal administration 'had cut the budget appropriation for maintaining flood defences by 50 per cent, so that for the first time in 37 years Louisiana was unable to supply the protection it knew it would need in the event of catastrophe'.

Suddenly, natural disasters appear to behave in the way only human-made, *moral* ills were previously supposed to. They are blatantly selective; one would say 'choosy' were one not afraid of being charged with an anthropomorphic fallacy. One could say it nevertheless and dismiss the charge, because it is equally blatant that the apparent selectivity of 'natural' blows comes from morally *pregnant*, even if not morally *motivated*, human action.

The protection of humanity against the blind caprices of nature was an integral part of the modern promise. The modern implementation of that project, however, has not made nature less blind and capricious, while focusing instead on the selective distribution of immunity against its effects. The modern struggle to disempower natural calamities follows the pattern of order-building and economic progress: whether by design or default, it divides humanity into those categories worthy of care and the *unwertes Leben* – the lives unworthy of living. As a consequence, it also specializes in an uneven distribution of fears – whatever the specific cause of the fear in question might be.

Hurricanes, earthquakes and floods are not special cases. We have managed to render selective even that most unchoosy, truly universal of natural ills: the biological limitation of human life. As Max Hastings commented, modern wealth offers its possessors every chance of living to a ripe old age. Until the twentieth century, disease was no respecter of purses. The wife of a Victorian financial colossus was almost as vulnerable to the perils of childbirth as a maid in his household. The tombstones of the great reveal how many died long before their natural spans were exhausted.

Today medical science can do extraordinary things for people able to pay. There has never been a wider gulf between the remedies available to the rich and those on offer to most of the poor, even in societies with advanced healthcare systems.[8]

Whether it is aimed at disasters of natural or artificial origin, the outcome of the modern war on human fears seems to be their *social redistribution* rather than any *reduction in volume*.

The emerging habit of speaking of the tsunami, Katrina or other natural disasters in terms of a calamity that could have been averted – in the way we used to discuss the consequences of human miscalculation or negligence – is itself a most intriguing phenomenon, a sign of a watershed in modern history whose significance is worth pondering carefully. It signals a surprising meeting between the ideas of 'natural' disasters and social/moral ones (that is, those gestated and/or perpetrated by humans); between two kinds of catastrophe that had been held wide apart throughout the history of modernity . . .

Susan Neiman, the author – already quoted – of a fundamental study of the succession of competing images and interpretations of evil in modern history,[9] goes as far as to suggest that the strict separation of the concepts of natural and social disasters, earlier inseparably mixed in the idea of God's will – a separation that took place in the course of the heated debates triggered by the 1755 Lisbon earthquake and fire – marks the real *beginning* of 'the modern'

> precisely for its attempt to divide responsibility clearly . . . If Enlightenment is the courage to think for oneself, it's also the courage to assume responsibility for the world into which one is thrown. Radically separating what earlier ages called natural from moral evils was thus part of the meaning of modernity.

And yet her winding up of the story of the modern challenge sounds nothing like its boisterous and emboldening beginning:

Modern conceptions of evil were developed in the attempt to stop blaming God for the state of the world, and to take responsibility for it on our own. The more responsibility for evil was left to the human, the less worthy the species seemed to take it on. We are left without direction. Returning to intellectual tutelage isn't an option for many, but hopes for growing up now seem void.

One wonders which one of the two evils, the *natural* or the *social* (and thus eligible to be registered as a *moral* fault), had to cover a longer distance to make their reunion possible and to reach once more, after a separation of two and a half centuries, the point of encounter and merger with its counterpart.

The 'natural' evil had to renounce its 'naturalness', that feature which cast 'nature', in opposition to 'culture', as a phenomenon definitely *not* of human creation and thereby placed firmly beyond human power to challenge, to tinker with, to rearrange or reform. Culture, nature's opponent, however did not treat any of the successively drawn boundaries of nature, simultaneously products and determinants of culture's own self-limitation, as anything more than temporary armistice lines, definitely negotiable and breakable. From the beginning of the modern era, culture was bent on following Voltaire's formula: 'the secret of arts is to correct nature'. Once the opposition between 'nature' and 'culture' was proclaimed, the area which 'nature' was reluctantly allowed to rule never stopped shrinking, turning bit by bit into a 'negative derivative' of culture: an artefact of a regrettable delay in the discovery of successive 'secrets of art'. Somewhere at the end of the long road ahead loomed the vision of the time when the territory temporarily ceded to 'nature' would be fully conquered, absorbed into the domain of 'culture' and subjected as a whole to exclusively human management (and consequently passing into the domain of human responsibility); becoming thereby indistinguishable from the realm that was open and amenable to human design and purposeful 'correction' (but also vulnerable, as was bound to become clear later, to human blunders deriving from wrong motives or negligence).

In order presently to return to a point of meeting and blending with natural disasters, social/moral evil had, on the other hand, to acquire all the features of its counterpart/opposition of which it had been thoroughly and emphatically stripped at the moment of its conceptual birth: the tendency to strike at random, to affect guilty and innocent alike, to be impossible or at least exceedingly difficult to anticipate, and to stay beyond human power to arrest it, let alone avert it. In other words, it had to assume the character of its alleged opposite, be a 'nature-like catastrophe': a sudden, abrupt and radical rupture in continuity, an unannounced entry of abnormality into the routine – but a rupture that had gestated and matured, albeit unnoticed and perhaps unnoticeable, inside that routine.

The itinerary along which natural disasters passed before they could reach a meeting point with the moral misdeed is easy to comprehend for people as modern as we are. It is sketched with a pen which we are all well trained to use. Its story is told in the words all too familiar to us: in the language of boundary breaking, invasion, conquest, annexation, colonization. That itinerary was anticipated, and intended, from the start. At least since Francis Bacon, its destination – complete human mastery over nature – was fixed; only the timing was, reluctantly, left hostage to the vagaries of fate – though it was hoped that, as the conquest progressed and the ransom needing to be paid came ever closer to nil, the extent of the residual hazards of 'blind fate' would be radically tapered.

On the other hand, the itinerary of moral guilt must have taken modern men and women by surprise. It went against the grain of everything the modern spirit stood for: in stark opposition to common expectations, hopes and intentions, and far from eliminating the vexing randomness, contingency and incomprehension from the human condition, it reintroduced and reasserted the haphazard, the purposeless and the unpredictable, and settled them in the areas of human presence-in-the-world where the strongest battalions and most trusted weapons of the self-assured conquerors and would-be masters of nature were deployed. While waging war against the inhuman caprices of nature, modernity to its horror ended up exposing to the arbitrariness of a nature-like chaos the 'soft underbelly' of human enterprise: the management of human cohabitation, assumed to be the obvious and uncontested realm of human reason, know-how and industry.

At the threshold of the modern era, the millennia-long armistice and uneasy cohabitation between nature in God's disguise and its human creatures was broken, and a front line was drawn between nature and humanity. The two modalities were seen as all but incompatible. To humanity, ever more eloquent and ambitious, guided by purpose and bent on forcing the world to serve its ambitions, nature now stood opposed, as a Cartesian object stands to a thinking subject: inert, devoid of purpose, obstreperous, numb and indifferent to human aspirations.

As long as it confronted humans in the guise of an omnipotent yet benevolent God, nature was a mystery that defied human comprehension: indeed, it was hard to square God's benevolence-cum-omnipotence with the profusion of evil in a world which He himself had designed and set in motion. The solution to that quandary most commonly offered – that natural disasters visited on humanity were just punishments visited on moral sinners – could not account for the stark evidence summarized by Voltaire in the poem he composed to commemorate the 1755 Lisbon earthquake and fire: 'l'innocent, ainsi que le coupable, / subit également ce mal inévitable' (the innocent, as well as the guilty, were equally subjected to this unavoidable blow). This mind-boggling quandary (vividly articulated, let me repeat, more than two millennia earlier in the Book of Job, the story of how the most illustrious sages of the time racked their brains in vain attempts to explain why nature, God's obedient creation and tool, should strike Job – an exemplary embodiment of virtue, piety and loyalty to God's commandments – with a most exquisite assortment of evils) haunted the *philosophes* of emergent modernity just as it had generations of theologians. The evident profligacy of evil in the world could not be reconciled with the combination of benevolence and omnipotence imputed to the world's maker and supreme manager.

The contradiction could not be resolved; it could only be taken off the agenda by what Max Weber described as the *Entzäuberung* ('disenchantment') of nature, singling this out as the true birth-act of the 'modern spirit' – that is, by the hubris grounded in the new 'we can do it, we will do it' attitude of self-confidence. In a sort of a penalty for the inefficacy of obedience, prayer and the practice of virtue (the three instruments recommended and hoped to evoke the desired responses from a benevolent and omnipotent Divine Subject), nature was stripped of subjecthood, and so of the very *capacity* of choosing between benevolence and malice. However impotent, humans could still hope to ingratiate themselves in God's eyes and could even protest God's verdicts and argue and negotiate their case; trying to debate and bargain with 'disenchanted' nature in the hope of currying its graces was evidently pointless.

Apart from the disposal of the irritating, logic-defying aporia, the disenchantment (or, more to the point, the 'de-divination' or just 'desecration') of nature brought another, staggeringly powerful effect: emancipation from the most awesome of fears – from the horror of hopelessness in the face of evil, deriving from the absence of tools and skills equal to the task of fighting evil back and keeping it at a safe distance.

Threats did not disappear, of course, and stripped of its Divine disguise disenchanted nature appeared no less tremendous, menacing and terror-inspiring than before; but what the prayers had failed to accomplish, science-supported *techne* – targeted at dealing with blind and numb nature, though not with an omniscient and speaking God – surely would, once it accumulated the skills to do things and used them to have things done. One could now expect the randomness and unpredictability of nature to be only a temporary irritant, and believe that the prospect of forcing nature to obey the will of humans was just a matter of time. *Natural* disasters might (and should!) be subjected to the same fate as *social* ills, which with due skill and effort could obviously be exiled from the human world and barred from returning. Discomforts caused by nature's antics would be eventually dealt with just as effectively as those calamities brought about by human malice and wantonness. Sooner or later, *all* threats, natural and moral alike, would become predicable and preventable, obedient to the power of reason; how soon that would happen depended solely on the determination with which the powers of human reason were deployed. Nature would become just like those other aspects of the human condition that are evidently made by humans, and so in principle manageable and 'correctible'. As Immanuel Kant's categorical imperative implied – deploying reason, our inalienable endowment, we can raise the kind of behaviour we would wish to become universal to the rank of *natural law*.

This was how it was hoped – at the start of the modern era and through a good part of its history – that human affairs would develop. As present experience suggests, however, they were really developing in the opposite direction. Rather than promoting

reason-guided behaviour to the rank of natural law, its consequences were degraded to the level of irrational nature. Natural
catastrophes did not become more like moral misdeeds, 'manageable in principle'; it was on the contrary the lot of immorality to
become or be revealed to be ever more similar to 'classic' natural
catastrophes: hazardous like them, unpredictable, unpreventable,
incomprehensible and immune to human reason and wishes.
Disasters brought about by human actions arrive from an opaque
world, strike at random, in places impossible to anticipate, and
escape or defy the kind of explanation which sets human actions
apart from all other events: explanation by *motives* or *purposes*.
Above all – the evil caused by the immoral actions of humans
appears ever more unmanageable *in principle*.

Let me restate the case which will now be argued in more detail:
the wholly unanticipated but ominous reshaping of social/moral
catastrophes in the likeness of unmanageable natural disasters
was, paradoxically, an unintended yet in all probability unavoidable product of the modern struggle to render the world transpar-
ent, predictable, regular, continuous and manageable.

If the moral disasters of our times escape explanations in terms
of motives and purposes, it is thanks to the triumphs scored by
an alliance of the modern spirit, know-how, capacity to act and
resourcefulness in their war against the interference of notoriously
capricious human intentions in the grand design of a reason-
dictated, orderly world, desired to be immune to all disequilibrat-
ing pressures. That war had to be waged, explicitly or not, against
the selfsame autonomous human agency which was ostensibly to
emerge reinforced from the modern transformations.

The war strategy was twofold, though its two precepts were
mutually dependent and reinvigorating.

It consisted, first, of the 'adiaphorization' tendency: the tendency to play down the relevance of moral criteria, or whenever
possible to eliminate such criteria altogether from an evaluation
of the desirability (or indeed permissibility) of human actions,
leading ultimately to individual human agents being expropriated
of their moral sensitivity and their moral impulses being
repressed.

It consisted, secondly, of individual human agents being expropriated of moral responsibility for the consequences of their deeds

– as if translating into secular terms Martin Luther's precept (repeatedly quoted by Max Weber in pondering the nature of modern times) that 'the Christian does what is right and places the outcome in God's hands'.[10]

The principal instrument of the twin arts of adiaphorization and emancipation from responsibility was (or rather aimed to become, though never with complete success) modern bureaucracy. It strove to place the office off-limits to human emotions, to spiritual bonds stretching beyond the office walls, to loyalties to purposes other than those officially authorized, and to rules of conduct recommended by authorities other than the office statute books. Loyalty to the *esprit de corps* was to be enough to ground the ethical code regulating the totality of bureaucratic procedure; as with all other ethical codes claiming endorsement from on high, it neither tolerated competition nor allowed renegotiation. Bureaucracy required *conformity to the rule*, not a *moral judgement*. Indeed, the morality of the officer was redefined as obedience to command and a readiness to see the job well done – whatever the nature of the job commanded to be done and whatever its impact on those at the receiving end of bureaucratic action. Bureaucracy was a contraption serving the task of *ethical deskilling*.

The performance of an organization managing to come close to the ideal type of bureaucracy would be independent of whatever might still remain of the moral conscience of its officers. And since bureaucracy stood for the supreme embodiments of rationality and order, it also targeted morally inspired behaviour as opposed to, or even incompatible with, the idea of order and the precepts of reason.

Bureaucracy excelled as well in freeing the executors of the task from responsibility for its outcomes and repercussions. It effectively replaced 'responsibility *for*' with 'responsibility *to*': responsibility for an action's impact on its object with responsibility to the superior, the command-giver. As all but one of the superiors were agents of their own superiors, who either gave or passed on the command and monitored its fulfilment, for most if not all office incumbents and at most if not all levels of the bureaucratic hierarchy the origins of the command and the authority endorsing the duty to obey receded into a distant and misty 'up there' – with double effect: first (to recall Hannah Arendt felicitous phrase), a 'floating' of responsibility, making it all but impossible to locate and ascribe it precisely, turning it for all practical purposes into 'nobody's' responsibility; and second, an investment of the duty to follow orders with an absolute, since irresistible power not much inferior to the strength of Divine commands.

The necessity of unquestioned obedience to commands was argued in terms of instrumental rationality. In fact, though, another rationality, quite opposite to the official version, and seldom if ever vented in public (and perhaps for that reason absent from Max Weber's four-item list of legitimations deployed to justify the claim of those in a position of power to obedience), put modern development into operation and to a large extent determined the crucial choices made along its course. Rather than searching for and selecting the most effective and likely means to achieve the goals set, that other, 'latent' rationality, *dictated* by instruments rather than just *dictating* instruments, sought the most profitable objectives to which the available means could be turned. In that rationality, the *means*, not the *ends*, were the invariants of the equation, being the sole 'hard facts' available; it was the *purposes* of action, not its *tools*, that were eminently variable and pliable. While the low status accorded to value judgement in modern thought was explained by reference to the fact that the 'is' does not determine the 'ought', and entrenched through the postulate of 'value-free' inquiry and 'value-neutral' knowledge, in reality something very different was happening: the purpose was sought and chosen in practice as a derivative of the available means. The 'is' of the available means was allowed to determine the 'ought' of the goal choosers, and it did so all the more effectively thanks to the denial of the autonomous status and authority of values, the refuting of separate criteria by which objectives of action needed to or had to be judged and selected, and a *de facto* exemption of values from the domain of reason-guided inquiry.

The efforts to denigrate moral judgements and eliminate them from the decision-making process as irrelevant brought in their wake a considerable weakening of the power of moral judgement – a development that made decision-makers simultaneously free and helpless to select the ways in which instruments were to be used. With the fading of the skills required by the task of value choice due to the diminished interest and concern in values, and with the task itself devalued, decisions as to how and to what purpose the currently available instruments of effective action should be deployed had to be all but arbitrary.

Dupuy recalls the sombre prediction recorded in 1948 by John von Neumann, the pioneer theorist of automatons and computers:[11] soon we, the constructors of automatic machines, will be as defenceless in the face of our creation as we are when confronted with complex natural phenomena. The time that has elapsed since has fully confirmed the soundness of Neumann's premonition. The new technology brought into being in the last half-century behaves – 'grows', 'develops' – just as nature does. The apparitions of motive, intention, design, destination, direction all emerge out of haphazard movements of 'completely blind mechanisms', and there is no way of being sure that the movements will lead us in a 'good direction', and no guarantee whatsoever that they won't lead us into a blind alley or an abyss. All of this, Dupuy concludes, is happening as if *human-made* technology, acquiring yet stronger independence and self-propelling momentum with every step it takes, is turning into an *inhuman* force destined to relieve its human inventors of the burden of freedom and autonomy . . .

If the bureaucracy of the solid modern era actively 'adiaphorized' the morally pregnant effects of human actions, the emancipated technology of our liquid modern times obtains similar effects through an 'ethical tranquillization' of sorts. It offers ostensible short-cut exits for moral impulses and quick-fix solutions for ethical quandaries, while relieving the actors from responsibility for both, shifting that responsibility to technical artefacts and, in the long run, 'morally deskilling' the actors, putting their moral conscience to sleep, grooming insensitivity to the full impact of moral challenges and, all in all, morally disarming the actors when it comes to difficult choices requiring a measure of self-denial or self-sacrifice. Particularly when mediated by consumer markets, the *soi-disant* 'technological fetishism' translates moral choices into acts of selecting the right commodities – implying that all moral impulses can be unloaded and all ethical problems resolved, or at least simplified and made easy, with the help of the products of the biotechnical, bioengineering or pharmaceutical industries. 'Ethical tranquillization' comes in a package deal with a clear conscience and moral blindness.

The fear which the ambiguities of the moral condition and the ambivalences of moral choices tend to arouse is not thereby put to rest. On the contrary, it tends to be magnified as it is shifted away from a direct confrontation and focused on technological processes which moral actors ill understand and whose dynamics they cannot penetrate, let alone control. The price to pay for the 'ethical tranquillizers' is the transfer of ethical command into the realm of the 'great unknown', where catastrophes gestate which are beyond the power of humans to predict and fight back against.

Jodi Dean has recently analysed new aspects added to 'technological fetishism' with the advent and spread of electronic communication and electronically mediated 'networks'.[12] She suggests 'the wired revolutionaries' could now 'think that they were changing the world comforted all the while that nothing would really change (or, at best, they could get record companies to lower the prices on compact discs)'.

> The technological fetish 'is political' for us, enabling us to go about the rest of our lives relieved of the guilt that we might not be doing our part and secure in the belief that we are after all informed, engaged citizens. The paradox of the technological fetish is that the technology acting in our stead actually enables us to remain politically passive. We don't have to assume political responsibility because, again, technology is doing it for us . . .
> The 'fix' lets us think that all we need is to universalize a particular technology, and then we will have a democratic or reconciled social order.

No wonder, we can add, that when it is brought to us (often brutally) that our expectations have been dashed and that what was expected and hoped for failed to happen, the effect is as shocking as are the impacts of natural catastrophes. And the repressed suspicion that the technology to which our hopes have been entrusted may frustrate or destroy those hopes is an added and formidable source of fear.

Here, I would guess, lies the deepest cause of that largely unplanned, random and hazardous course of modern development which probably inspired Jacques Ellul to suggest that technology (the skills and tools of action) develops just because it develops, needing no other cause or motive. A few years earlier than Ellul, in *The Human Condition* written shortly after the end of war and published in 1958, Hannah Arendt warned that we, terrestrial creatures bidding for cosmic significance, will shortly be unable to comprehend and articulate the things we are capable of doing; and a few years later Hans Jonas complained that while we can now affect by our actions spaces and times so distant as to be unknown and incomprehensible to us, our moral sensitivity has hardly progressed since the time of Adam and Eve.

All three great thinkers conveyed a similar message: we suffer from a *moral lag*. Motives for action tend to be clearly visualized only as afterthoughts, often in the capacity of a retrospective apology or a case for extenuating circumstances, while the actions we take, while sometimes inspired by moral insights or impulses, are most commonly prompted by the resources at our disposal. As the *spiritus movens* of our actions, cause has taken over from the intention.

Fifty years ago Alfred Schütz, a faithful follower of Weber's 'understanding sociology' programme rooted in the modern view of humans as purpose-guided creatures, set about unmasking the self-deception manifested in the all-too-commonly deployed 'I did it *because*' formula, and insisted that the actions of the inveterately goal-pursuing human creatures should be more correctly described in terms of 'I did it *in order to*'. An opposite injunction would be in order nowadays however, as the goals, particularly the ethically meaningful goals, tend to be increasingly ascribed to our actions *ex post facto*.

In such an *ex post facto* mode the decisions to unleash the murderous power of atomic bombs on Hiroshima on 6 August 1945 and three days later on Nagasaki have been justified in their aftermath by the need to force Japan into immediate capitulation and thereby to save the lives of innumerable soldiers who would otherwise have died in the attempt to invade the Japanese archipelago. The court of history is still sitting, but that official retrospective explanation is being challenged by a number of American historians as being at odds with the facts of the time. What the critics assert is that as early as July 1945 Japan was close to capitulation. There remained only two conditions to be met to prompt Japan to surrender: that Truman should agree to the Soviets joining the war on Japan immediately, and that the allies sitting at the Potsdam conference should promise that the Mikado would be allowed to remain on the throne after Japan's surrender.

Truman stalled however and refused his consent once he had received, shortly after his arrival in Potsdam (on 17 July exactly), the report from Alamogordo in New Mexico that the atomic bomb had been successfully tested and that the results of the test 'were yet more impressive than expected'. Wary of letting the new and exorbitantly costly technological contraption go to waste, Truman was obviously playing for time. The stakes for which that game of procrastination was played became apparent from Truman's triumphant announcement reported by the *New York Times* on 7 August 1945: 'we have made the most audacious scientific bet in human history, a bet of more than two billion dollars, and we've won.' Two billion dollars should not go to waste . . . And so they did not.

On 16 March 1945, when Germany was already on its knees and to all practical intents and purposes the war was won, a British air force commander, Arthur 'Bomber' Harris, sent 225 Lancasters and 11 Mosquitos to unload 289 tons of high explosives and 573 tons of incendiary bombs on Würzburg, a modest-sized town of 107,000 inhabitants, rich in arts and history but rather poor in industry. Between 9.20 and 9.37 p.m. about 5,000 of the town's residents were killed (of which 66 per cent were female, 14 per cent children) and 21,000 houses destroyed, so that only 6,000 of the survivors could remain inside the city after the bombing. Hermann Knell, who researched the archives and collated all these data,[13] asks why a town clearly devoid of strategic significance (a fact obliquely admitted by the official history of the RAF bomber campaign against Germany, in which Würzburg did not get a mention, being thereby reduced to the status of another 'collateral casualty' of war) was selected as a target. Having explored and ruled out one by one all the alternative answers, Knell settled for the sole sensible explanation: 'Arthur Harris, the RAF Bomber Command Chief, and Carl Spaatz, Commander of the US Air Force stationed in Britain and Italy, had run out of worthwhile targets by early 1945.'

> The bombing progressed as planned without consideration of the changed military situation. The destruction of German cities continued until the end of April. Seemingly once the military machine was moving it could not be stopped. It had a life of its own. There

was now all the equipment and soldiers on hand. It must have been that aspect that made Harris decide to have Würzburg attacked . . .

But why Würzburg of all places? Purely a question of convenience. As previous reconnaissance flights had shown, 'the city could be easily located with the electronic aids available at the time'. And the city was sufficiently distanced from the advancing allied troops to stave off the risk of another 'friendly fire' (that is, showering bombs on one's own troops). In other words, Würzburg was 'an easy and riskless target'.[14] This was its unintended fault, a kind for which no target would ever be pardoned once 'the military machine was moving'.

At the far end of the great leap to freedom recorded in history under the name of the 'modern era', we are no less, and apparently more, the 'creatures of determination' than we were at its start – though this time as a result of a detour (the longest of all detours, a true 'mother of detours', their enabling cause and pattern to be endlessly replicated, a genuinely meta-detour) which can be retrospectively described as a bid to substitute, in the role of the determinant-in-chief of our determined condition, our technological potency and our knowledge in place of the powers of nature and our ignorance. We are to nature what the sorcerer's apprentice was to his master. Just like that hot-headed, bold though not particularly circumspect youngster, we have grasped the secret of setting free and unleashing pent-up forces and have resolved to use them *before* we have had the chance to learn how to stop them. And we are horrified by the thought that, perhaps, with the forces set in motion and allowed to develop their own momentum, it is too late to search for the magic incantations capable of taming them again.

The irony of it all is that, whether at the starting point or the far end of the grand detour, we find ourselves in a strikingly similar plight: confused, bewildered, unsure of *what* is to be done and *how* and *by whom* it could be done were we to know what that must be. Like our ancestors, we are overwhelmed by fears oozing from the vast void between the grandiosity of the challenge and the paucity and flimsiness of our tools and resources – though this time we don't truly believe that sooner rather than later the void can be bridged. We experience what people must have felt when they were overwhelmed by Mikhail Backtin's 'cosmic fear': the awe and trembling caused by the sublime and tremendous, by the sight of giant mountains and boundless seas evidently immune to human efforts to scale them and blind and deaf to human cries for mercy. This time, though, it is not the mountains and the seas, but human-made artefacts and their impenetrable by-products and side-effects that exude the most sinister of our fears.

Before this point had been reached (or rather before we realized that this was the case) our ancestors hoped that the discrepancy between the size of the challenge and our ability to counter or foil it was a temporary nuisance, that the road they were walking led forward, and that through persisting in following that road they and we, their successors, would leave the fears of inadequacy behind. They took that road not knowing it to be only a detour, and unaware that it would eventually bring us back to the condition they wished to escape.

The sole, but formidable difference between the starting and the finishing points of that grand detour is that we are now returning from travels with the loss of our *illusions*, though not our *fears*. We have tried to exorcise our fears away, and failed, having only added in the course of our trial to the sum total of the horrors that clamour to be confronted and chased away. *The most gruesome among the added fears is the fear of being incapable of averting or escaping the condition of being afraid.* With the initial optimism gone, we are now afraid that the catastrophes that frightened our ancestors are not only bound to be repeated, but are also inescapable.

We fear what we can't manage. We call that inability to manage 'incomprehension'; what we call 'comprehension' of something is our know-how for tackling it. That knowledge of how to handle things, that *comprehension*, is a 'free gift' attached to (or rather built into) the tools that are capable of doing the handling. As a rule, that knowledge comes as an afterthought; it resides, we may say, first in the tools and only later settles in minds through reflection on the effects of using them. In the absence of tools and the practices enabled by the tools, such knowledge – such 'comprehension' – is unlikely to appear. *Comprehension is born of the ability to manage.* What we are *not* able to manage is 'unknown' to us;

and the 'unknown' is frightening. *Fear is another name we give to our defencelessness.*

It may be argued that in addition to the factors spelled out earlier, there has been one departure which in recent years has brought home the awesome might of what we can/must describe as the sphere of the unknown, incomprehensible, unmanageable. Up to now, that fateful departure has been referred to under the name of 'globalization'.

4

Terrors of the Global

Thus far, ours is a wholly *negative* globalization: unchecked, unsupplemented and uncompensated for by a 'positive' counterpart which is still a distant prospect at best, though according to some prognoses already a forlorn chance. Allowed a free run, 'negative' globalization specializes in breaking those boundaries too weak to withstand the pressure, and in drilling numerous, huge and unplugable holes through those boundaries that successfully resist the forces bent on dismantling them.

The 'openness' of our open society has acquired a new gloss these days, one undreamt of by Karl Popper, who coined that phrase. No longer a precious yet frail product of brave, though stressful, self-assertive efforts, it has become instead an irresistible fate brought about by the pressures of formidable extraneous forces; a side-effect of 'negative globalization' – that is, the highly selective globalization of trade and capital, surveillance and information, coercion and weapons, crime and terrorism, all now disdaining territorial sovereignty and respecting no state boundary.

If the idea of an 'open society' originally stood for the self-determination of a free society proud of its openness, it now brings to most minds the terrifying experience of heteronomous, vulnerable populations overwhelmed by forces they neither control nor truly understand, horrified by their own undefendability and obsessed with the security of their borders and of the population inside them – since it is precisely that security *inside* borders and *of* borders that eludes their grasp and seems bound to stay beyond their reach forever (or as least as long as the planet is subjected to solely *negative* globalization, which all too often seems to be the same thing). On a globalized planet, populated by the forcibly 'opened' societies, security cannot be gained, let alone reliably assured, in one country or in a selected group of countries: not by their own means, and not independently of the state of affairs in the rest of the world.

Neither can justice, that preliminary condition of lasting peace. The perverted 'openness' of societies enforced by negative globalization is itself the prime cause of injustice and so, obliquely, of conflict and violence. As Arundhati Roy puts it, 'while the elite pursue their voyages to their imaginary destination, some place at the top of the world, the poor have been caught into a spiral of crime and chaos.'[1] It was the actions of the United States together with its various satellites, like the World Bank, the International Monetary Fund and the World Trade Organization, that 'prompted subsidiary developments, dangerous sub-products such as nationalism, religious fanaticism, fascism, and of course terrorism, advancing marching step in step with the neoliberal project of globalization'. 'Market without boundaries' is a recipe for injustice, and ultimately for a new world disorder in which (contrary to Clausewitz) it is the politics that becomes a continuation of war by other means. *Global lawlessness and armed violence feed each other*, mutually reinforce and reinvigorate; as the ancient wisdom warns – *inter arma silent leges* (when arms speak, laws keep silent). The globalization of harm and damage rebounds in the globalization of resentment and vengeance.

Negative globalization has done its job, and all societies are now fully and truly open, materially and intellectually, so that any injury from deprivation and indolence, wherever it happens, comes complete with the insult of injustice: the feeling of a wrong having been done, a wrong yelling to be repaired, but first of all avenged . . . And, in Milan Kundera's succinct summary, such 'unity of mankind' as has been brought about by globalization means primarily that 'there is nowhere one can escape to'.[2] No secure shelters left where one can hide. In the liquid modern world, the dangers and fears are also liquid-like – or are they rather gaseous? They flow, seep, leak, ooze . . . No walls have been invented yet to stop them, though many try to build them.

The spectre of vulnerability hovers over the 'negatively globalized' planet. We are all in danger, and we are all dangers to each
other. There are only three roles to play – perpetrators, victims,
and 'collateral casualties' – and for the first role there is no shortage of bidders, while the ranks of those cast as the second and
the third grow unstoppably. Those of us already on the receiving
end of negative globalization frantically seek escape and breathe
vengeance. Those as yet spared are frightened that their turn to
do the same may – and will – come.

On a planet tightly wrapped in the web of human interdependence, there is nothing the *others* do or can do of which we may
be sure that it won't affect *our* prospects, chances and dreams.
There is nothing *we* do or desist from doing of which we may say
with confidence that it won't affect the prospects, chances and
dreams of some *others* whom we don't know or even know of. It
is common now to discuss our new condition of universal and
all-embracing connectedness and interdependence in terms of
risks and unanticipated consequences – but one wonders whether
the concept of 'risk' grasps and conveys the true novelty inserted
into the human condition by one-sidedly negative globalization.

The idea of 'risk' restates obliquely, and tacitly reaffirms, the
presumption of an essential regularity of the world. Only on such
an assumption can risks be in principle, true to their definition,
calculated – and only as long as such an assumption holds can
one try, with a degree of success, to minimize them through acting
or refraining from action. The snag, however, is that the probability of defeat, harm or another calamity may be calculated – and
so the suffering they would cause may also be avoided or at least
reduced – only in as far as the law of great numbers applies to
their occurrence (the greater their frequency, the more precise and
reliable are the calculations of their probability). In other words,
the concept of 'risks' makes sense only in a *routinized*, monotonous and repetitive world, in which causal sequences recur often
and commonly enough for the costs and benefits of intended
actions and their chances of success and failure to be amenable
to statistical processing and be judged by reference to precedents;
in a world to which John Stuart Mill's canons of induction apply
thanks to steadily growing records of similar causal sequences
zeroing in on a steady distribution of probabilities.

This is not, however, what the 'negatively globalized' world is like. In such a world as ours, the effects of actions spread far beyond the reach of the routinizing impact of control and beyond the scope of the knowledge needed to design it. What makes our world vulnerable are principally the dangers of *non-calculable* probability, a thoroughly different phenomenon from those to which the concept of 'risk' commonly refers. *Dangers that are non-calculable in principle arise in a setting that is irregular in principle*, where broken sequences and the non-repetition of sequences become a rule, and normlessness a norm. They are *uncertainty under a different name.*

Possibly, the present kind of planetary uncertainty is bound to remain incurable until such time as negative globalization is supplemented and tamed by the positive sort and probabilities once more become amenable to calculation. The roots of our vulnerability are of a *political* and *ethical* nature.

In the classic and by now canonical formulation by Hans Jonas, introduced in *The Imperative of Responsibility*, the ethical imagination has failed, and is still failing, to catch up with the fast expanding realm of our ethical responsibilities. One can hear reverberating in that formulation the same concerns that haunted Jean-Paul Sartre's oeuvre ('whatever we do, we take responsibility for something, but we don't know what that something is'). The dense network of interdependence makes us all *objectively* responsible (that is, responsible whether we know it or not, whether we like it or not, and – an ethically crucial point – whether we intend it or not) for each other's miseries; our moral imagination, however, has been historically shaped to deal only with others who reside inside a circle of spatial and temporal proximity, within sight and touch – and it has not as yet notably advanced beyond that traditional (endemic?) limitation. We may add that the advent of 'information highways', and so of an electronically mediated *tele*-proximity, may be a stimulus towards such an advancement – but to catch up with the scope of objective responsibility already attained an 'institutional stretch' still needs to be laid, paved and policed. Such a stretch is still stuck at the drawing-board stage; worse still, for all we know construction work is unlikely to start as long as the conditions of negative globalization prevail.

If anything, the gap between the extent of our objective responsibility and the responsibility accepted, assumed and practised is presently widening rather than being bridged. The prime reason for the impotence of the latter to embrace the whole scope of the former is, as Jean-Pierre Dupuy suggests,[3] the traditionally self-restricting tendency of the orthodox formula of normative responsibility to rely heavily on the concepts of 'intent' and 'motive', which are totally inadequate to cope with the present challenge of a planet-wide interdependence (and we may comment that the absence of a system of similarly planet-wide law and of planet-wide jurisdiction, its executive arm, makes the prospect of such coping even more nebulous). 'The distinction', Dupuy says, 'between a killing by an intentional individual act' and killing as a result of 'the egoistic citizens of rich countries focusing their concerns on their own well-being while the others die of hunger' is becoming less and less tenable. Desperate searches for 'motive' in the style of detectives and policemen, in order to determine suspects and locate the perpetrator of a crime, will be to no avail when it comes to pinpointing the misdemeanours responsible for the present plight of the planet.

There is one more substantive difference between 'risks' and the present-day 'uncertainty' in addition to those already discussed. Risks that matter most and most need to be reckoned with grow thicker the closer they are, spatially and temporally, to the actors and their actions. Uncertainties, however, are spread in an exactly opposite fashion; they expand and thicken the further away the eyes move from the actor and the action. As the *spatial* distance grows, so does the complexity and density of the mesh of influences and interaction; as the *temporal* distance grows, so does the impenetrability of the future, that notoriously unknowable, 'absolute' other. Hence the paradox noted by Jonas – a paradox he struggled in vain to resolve: the effects of our actions, now reaching far into the life conditions of as yet unborn generations, demand unprecedented circumspection and an immense power of foresight; a power that nevertheless seems unattainable – not because of rectifiable and so hopefully transient faults in our cognitive faculties and efforts, but due to the essential and *in*curable aleatoriness of the future (of the 'not yet'). The impact of the resulting contingencies expands at an exponential pace with every step our imagination takes as it stretches to catch up with the ever longer duration of the direct results and side-effects of our decisions. Even the tiniest modification of the initial conditions, or a minuscule departure from the early developments anticipated, may result in a complete reversal of the end-states expected or hoped for.

This circumstance may not particularly trouble the risk managers; risks, after all, are pragmatically important as long as they remain calculable and so amenable to a cost-and-benefit assessment – and so, almost by definition, the only risks that are of any concern to the planners of action are those likely to affect the results within a relatively short space and time perspective. For ethics, however, in order to restore its past guiding potential in the present circumstances, it is necessary to accomplish precisely the opposite (to reach *beyond* the comfortingly cosy, since relatively familiar and in the short term regular realm), so that the above-mentioned aporia deriving from the nature of the present-day uncertainty (and ultimately from one-sided, negative globalization) is a major obstacle and fundamental worry.

Hence one more paradox in the liquid modern mosaics/kaleidoscope of paradoxes: as the capacity of our tools and resources for action grows, allowing us to reach ever further in space and time, so our fear grows of their inadequacy to eradicate the evil we see and the evil as yet unseen yet bound to be gestating . . . The most technologically equipped generation in human history is the generation most haunted by feelings of insecurity and helplessness. Or, as Robert Castel puts it in his incisive analysis of the current anxieties fed by insecurity,[4] we – at least in the developed countries – 'live undoubtedly in some of the most secure (*sûres*) societies that ever existed', and yet, contrary to the 'objective evidence', we – the most cosseted and pampered people of all – feel more threatened, insecure and frightened, more inclined to panic, and more passionate about everything related to security and safety than the people of most other societies on record . . .

Just how insecure we feel living on a negatively globalized planet, and how the 'moral lag' – responsible for the deepening contradiction between the remoteness of the effects of actions and the short range of the concerns that shape them – makes any escape from the state of endemic uncertainty, and the insecurity and fear it breeds, hardly conceivable, have been brought home in a highly dramatic way by the rise of global terrorism. 'The inconceivable, the unimaginable, had become brutally possible' is the way the meaning of its shocking discovery was summed up by Mark Danner, a professor of politics and journalism from Berkeley.[5]

Before sending troops to Iraq, Donald Rumsfeld declared that the 'war will be won when Americans feel secure again'.[6] But sending troops to Iraq pushed the mood of insecurity to new heights, in America and elsewhere. Far from shrinking, the spaces of lawlessness, the training grounds for global terrorism, expanded to unheard-of dimensions.

Four years have passed since Rumsfeld's decision, and terrorism has been gathering force – extensively and intensively – year by year. Terrorist outrages have been recorded in Tunisia, Bali, Mombasa, Riyadh, Istanbul, Casablanca, Jakarta, Madrid, Sharm el Sheikh and London; altogether, according to the State Department, there were 651 'significant terrorist attacks' in 2004 alone. Of those 198 – nine times more than the year before (not counting daily attacks on US troops) – in Iraq, to which the troops had been sent with a mission to put an end to the terrorist threat. In May 2005 there were ninety suicide bombings in Baghdad alone. Iraq, says Mark Danner, 'has become a grotesque advertisement for the power and efficacy of terror'.

As the most recent experience shows, the endemic ineffectiveness, or even outright counterproductiveness of military action against modern forms of terrorisms continue to be the rule. In the words of Michael Meacher, 'despite the "war on terror", over the past two years . . . al-Qaeda seems to have been more effective than in the two years before 9/11.' Adam Curtis goes a step further, suspecting that al-Qaeda barely existed at all except as a vague and diffused idea about 'cleansing a corrupt world through religious violence', and started life as an artefact of lawyers' action; it did not even have a name 'until early 2001, when the American government decided to prosecute Bin Laden in his absence and had to use anti-Mafia laws that required the existence of a named criminal organization'.[7] That suspicion sounds all the more credible as it becomes ever clearer that whatever else al-Qaeda may be, it does not answer the description of a cohesive, coordinated and structured organization. On 5 August 2005, Bush seems to have admitted that much, describing those responsible for terrorist atrocities and their acolytes as 'dark, dim and backwards' – referring perhaps, even if subconsciously, to the discovery that they have no equivalent of a Pentagon, no address where bombs and missiles can be unloaded in order to finish off, or at least paralyse for a time, their ability to plot and murder. No chain of command is there to be cut. There are no high ranks to be targeted so that the rank-and-file might feel lost and impotent.

In Mark Danner's opinion, 'Al Qaeda has now become Al Qaedaism' – a worldwide political movement – though rather than a tightly knit organization of the kind remembered from the solid modern past of the 'developed West', it looks more like 'an evolving, loose coalition of a score or so groups', with perpetrators of the terrorist assaults mostly 'homegrown' and not, strictly speaking, al-Qaeda; just 'spontaneous groups of friends', who have few links to any central leadership (and those they have are mostly internet mediated). And according to a later report,[8] the massive devastation of Falluja or Tal Afar, deemed to be headquarters of the insurgents, did not help. The Iraqi terrorists are notable for 'melting away ahead of gathering forces, only to set up planning and bomb-making cells in another hideaway'. 'The loosely knit and elusive networks . . . still can recruit' the discontented people whose numbers do nothing but grow in the aftermath of massive military assaults by the occupying forces. In the words of Brigadier-General Muhammad al-Askari of the Iraqi Ministry of Defence, 'there was little security forces could do to prevent another round of attacks . . . Any crazy guy anywhere in the world with weapons can create a catastrophe.' According to another *New York Times* report,[9] there were 126 car-bomb attacks in Baghdad alone in eighty days leading to 18 May 2005 – as against only twenty-five in the whole of 2004.

A 'senior officer' of the American troops in Iraq couldn't promise the press any firm prospects except his own belief that the campaign against the terrorists' insurgency in Iraq 'is going to succeed in the long run, even if it takes years, many years'. One wonders; after all, the 'war against terrorism', once limited to the intelligence services and the police, and now entrusted to the most powerful and best equipped army in the world, looks unwinnable. The military action in question tends so far to have the opposite effects to the declared intention. The most evident effect of the two 'anti-terrorist campaigns', in Afghanistan and in Iraq, has thus far been the establishment of two brand new global magnets,

greenhouses, powerhouses and training grounds for global terrorists, where the tactics of the 'anti-terrorist forces', their foibles and
weaknesses, are studied by the terrorists and their global recruits,
while new and yet more sophisticated outrages are plotted and
rehearsed before they are staged in the anti-terrorists' homes. As
Gary Younge observed some time ago,

> Tony Blair is not responsible for the more than 50 dead and 700
> injured on Thursday (5 July 2005). In all likelihood, 'jihadists' are.
> But he is partly responsible for the 100,000 people who have been
> killed in Iraq. And even at this early stage there is a far clearer
> logic linking these two events that there ever was tying Saddam
> Hussein to either 9/11 or weapons of mass destruction.[10]

As recently as 30 June 2005, three years after the anti-terrorist
campaign in Afghanistan, it was reported that

> violence has increased sharply in recent months, with a resurgent
> Taliban movement mounting daily attacks in southern Afghani-
> stan, gangs kidnapping foreigners and radical Islamists orch-
> estrating violent demonstrations against the government and
> foreign-financed organizations. The steady stream of violence has
> dealt a new blow to the still traumatized nation of 25 million. In
> dozens of interviews conducted in recent weeks around the country,
> Afghans voiced concerns that things are not improving, and that
> the Taliban and other dangerous players were gaining strength.[11]

A similar process has been set in motion in Iraq. News reports like
the one below, chosen at random, are brought day in, day out, differ-
ing from each other solely by the numbers of victims reported:

> The largest Iraqi-led counterinsurgency operation since the down-
> fall of Saddam Hussein set off a violent backlash on Sunday across
> Baghdad. At least 20 people were killed in the capital, 14 of them
> in a battle lasting several hours when insurgents initiated sustained
> attacks on several police stations and an army barracks . . . [E]ven
> moderate Sunni Arabs were wavering in the face of the new gov-
> ernment's sweeps.[12]

As for the state of mind of the top army commanders and the
population at large after the two-year long anti-terrorist actions
in Iraq:

The questions now are how many more times over how many years he [President Bush] might have to deliver the same message of patience and resolve – and whether the American public, confronted with the mounting death toll, an open-ended military commitment, lack of support from allies and a growing price tag, will accept it.

The [President Bush] speech offered no new policies or course corrections, and for the most part was a restatement of the ideas and language that he has been employing for two and a half years to explain the war . . . [13]

As a result of the enormous efforts, over more than two years, to catch or kill the armed terrorists and destroy their nests and breeding grounds, the 'anti-terrorist coalition' in Iraq is now further from its objective than at any earlier stage of the campaign. As the commanders of the expeditionary forces admit,[14] 'the sophistication of insurgent attacks' (averaging sixty-five a day!) grows, as well as 'the insurgents' ability to replenish their ranks as fast as they are killed'.

'We are capturing or killing a lot of insurgents,' said a senior Army intelligence officer, who spoke on condition of anonymity because he was not authorized to make his assessments public. 'But they're being replaced quicker than we can interdict their operations. There is always another insurgent ready to step up and take charge.'

At the same time, the Americans acknowledge that they are no closer to understanding the inner workings of the insurgency or stemming the flow of foreign fighters . . . [The insurgency] has largely eluded the understanding of American intelligence officers since the fall of Saddam Hussein's government 27 months ago.

The danger is that the violence [could leave] the community more embittered than ever and set the stage for even more violence and possibly civil war.

And as the punishing sallies by the Americans grow in ferocity, so the danger draws nearer. Another recent report informs us:

As the threat from bombs and suicide attacks has grown, the Pentagon has rushed 24,000 armored Humvees to Iraq since late 2003. But the insurgents have responded by building bombs powerful enough to penetrate the vehicles' steel plating . . .

'It's not realistic to think we will stop this,' says Sgt. Daniel McDonnell, who leads a three-man team of explosives technicians responsible for finding and defusing improvised explosive devices in Baghdad. 'We're fighting an enemy that goes home at night and doesn't wear uniforms. But we can get it to an acceptable level.'[15]

The snag is, though, that the ingenuity and the apparently inexhaustible resourcefulness of the terrorists forces their military opponents to lift the threshold of 'acceptability' higher almost by the day . . .

According to American military experts, the apparent proliferation of militant groups (about a hundred by recent estimates) 'offers perhaps the best explanation as to why the insurgency has been so hard to destroy'.[16] The rebels do not form an organization whose members 'dutifully carry out orders from above', but 'a far-flung collection of smaller groups that often act on their own or come together for a single attack'. The 'structure' (if one is permitted to use this term at all in their case) 'is horizontal as opposed to hierarchical, and ad hoc as opposed to unified'.

The same sources note yet another development in the terrorist strategy, which they take to be the explanation of the insurgents' 'ability to bring on recruits from around the Arab world' – namely, 'the reach and sophistication of [their] public relations'. Most of the terrorist groups, wary that their spectacular exploits might be overlooked by the broadcasters, are keen to cash in on the opportunities offered by the network of 'information highways' and 'regularly post updates of their exploits on the Web. Scarcely a day passes when one of the groups has not announced another attack with either a video or printed notice.'

Counting on appliances made available by the all-powerful globalizing pressures is an integral part of the terrorist strategy. In Mark Danner's words, the most powerful weapon of the nineteen terrorists who used their knives and box cutters to destroy Manhattan's Twin Towers was 'that most American of technological creation: the television set'. The worldwide notoriety promptly offered to the gory sights of even minor and comparatively inconsequential and insignificant terrorist acts can multiply their fear-inspiring potential, reaching the parts which the relatively scarce and often primitive and home-made arms at the terrorists' disposal (no comparison to the ample and high-tech weapons of their declared enemies) would never be able to reach, let alone seriously harm. That notoriety made possible by the worldwide television network and the web can also push the universal fears of vulnerability and the sense of ubiquitous danger far beyond the limits of the terrorists' own capacity.

True to its name, the paramount weapon of terrorism is sowing terror. And given the current state of the planet, rich crops are assured however inferior the quality of the seed.

Given the nature of contemporary terrorism, and above all the 'negatively globalized' setting in which it operates, the very notion of the 'war on terrorism' is all but a contradiction in terms.

Modern weapons, conceived and developed in the era of territorial invasions and conquests, are singularly unfit for locating, striking and destroying the extraterritorial, endemically elusive and eminently mobile targets, minute squads or just single men or women travelling light, armed with weapons that are easy to hide: they are difficult to pick out when they are on the way to another atrocity, and may perish in the place of the outrage or disappear from it as rapidly and inconspicuously as they arrived, leaving behind few if any clues of who they are. To deploy Paul Virilio's apt terms, we have now passed (an event only belatedly noted and grudgingly admitted by the military) from the times of 'siege warfare' to those of 'wars of movement'.[17] Given the nature of the modern weapons at the disposal of the military, responses to such terrorist acts are bound to appear awkward, clumsy and fuzzy, spilling over a much wider area than that affected by the terrorist outrage, and causing ever more numerous 'collateral casualties', and an ever greater volume of 'collateral damage', and so also more terror, disruption and destabilization than the terrorists could possibly have produced on their own – as well as provoking a further leap in the volume of accumulated grievance, hatred and pent-up fury and stretching still further the ranks of potential recruits to the terrorist cause. We may surmise that this circumstance is an integral part of the terrorists' design and the principal source of their strength, which exceeds many times the power of their numbers and arms.

Unlike their declared enemies, the terrorists need not feel constrained by the limits of the forces they themselves directly command. When working out their strategic designs and tactical plans, they may also include among their assets the probable, indeed almost certain reactions of the 'enemy', bound to magnify considerably the intended impact of their own atrocities. If the declared (immediate) purpose of the terrorists is to spread terror among the enemy population, then the enemy army and police, with the whole-hearted cooperation of the mass media, will certainly see to it that this purpose is achieved far beyond the level which the terrorists themselves would be capable of securing. And if the terrorists' long-term intention is to destroy human freedoms in liberal democracies and to 'close back' open societies, they may count again on the immense capacities commanded by the governments of the 'enemy countries'. A few packets of explosives and a few desperados eager to sacrifice their lives 'for the cause' can therefore go a long way – much, much further than the terrorists themselves could dream of achieving with the resources they themselves can muster, command and administer.

In the aftermath of the two terrorist outrages in London the *New York Times* concluded that in the light of recent developments in Britain and elsewhere it has become clear that 'the centrally controlled Al Quaeda of 9/11 is no more'. We are now confronting 'a new, more ominous face of terrorism in Europe'. Pierre de Bousquet, the director of DST, France's domestic intelligence service, points out that the terrorist groups are 'not homogeneous, but a variety of blends' – in other words they are formed ad hoc, recruited each time from different milieus and sometimes from quarters deemed mutually incompatible. They defy all categorial reasoning – rubbing the salt of incapacitating incomprehension into the wounds inflicted by the horrific deeds, and so adding more fear to the already frightening effects of the outrages. De Bousquet went on:

> Hard-core Islamists are mixing with petty criminals. People of different backgrounds and nationalities are working together. Some are European-born or have dual nationalities that make it easier for them to travel. The networks are much less structured than we used to believe. Maybe it's the mosque that brings them together, maybe it's prison, maybe it's the neighbourhood. And that makes it much more difficult to identify them and uproot them.[18]

Already in June 2004, speaking at a conference held in Florence, Peter Clarke (counterterrorism chief in Britain's police force) complained that 'if we take one or two leaders away, very quickly they are replaced and the network is reformed'. A fluid composition and rapidly shifting points of condensation are the attributes of this variety of 'nanotechnology'; torn tissue is patched back in no time and missing cells are replaced, while trackers are sent off the trail.

A confidential British government assessment of the threat presented by young British Muslim radicals (a memo prepared for the Prime Minister and disclosed by the *Sunday Times*) names two categories allied in the designing and perpetration of terrorist acts: 'well educated undergraduates' or those already 'with degrees and technical professional qualifications' in engineering or information technology, on the one hand, and 'underachievers with few or no qualifications, and often a criminal background', on the other. The authors of the document comment that 'Muslims are more likely than other faith groups to have no qualifications (over two-fifths have none) and to be unemployed and economically inactive, and are over-represented in deprived areas.'

But let us remember: negative globalization has done its job. However many border security guards, biometric appliances and explosive-sniffing dogs are deployed at the ports, borders that have already been thrown open and kept open by and for free-floating capital, commodities and information can't be sealed back and kept sealed against humans.

In the light of the evidence available thus far, we may surmise that when (if) terrorist acts eventually fizzle out, it will happen *despite* of and not *thanks* to the crude, sledgehammer violence of troops, which only fertilizes the soil on which terrorism blossoms and prevents the resolution of the social and political issues that alone could cut it off at its roots. Terrorism will fade and die out only when (if) its socio-political roots are cut. And that, alas, will take much more time and effort than a series of punitive military operations and even a set of thoroughly prepared policing actions.

The real – and *winnable* – war against terrorism is not conducted when the already half-ruined cities and villages of Iraq or Afghanistan are further devastated, but when the debts of poor countries are cancelled, when our rich markets are opened to their staple produce, when education is sponsored for the 115 million children currently deprived of access to any school, and when other similar measures are fought for, decided – and *implemented*.

Yet there are few if any encouraging signs that this truth has been understood, accepted and put into practice. The governments of the richest countries that gathered in Gleneagles in July 2005 allegedly to make poverty history are spending ten times more on arms between them than they spend on economic aid to Africa, Asia, Latin America and the poor countries of Europe taken together. Britain sets aside 13.3 per cent of its budget for armaments, spends 1.6 per cent on aid. For the US, the disproportion is still far greater: 25 per cent against 1 per cent.[19]

Indeed, one can only repeat after Meacher: more often than not, and most certainly after 11 September, we seem to be 'playing Bin Laden's game'. This is, as Meacher rightly insists, a lethally flawed policy. And an even less forgivable policy, I'd add, for not being really motivated by the intention to eradicate the terrorist scourge, let alone being preceded and accompanied by a sober analysis of the deep roots of the trouble and the wide range of undertakings needed to eradicate them. The 'lethally flawed policy' follows quite a different logic from the one which such an intention and such consideration would suggest. Meacher accuses the governments in charge of the 'war on terrorism' with

> unwillingness to contemplate what lies behind the hatred: why scores of young people are prepared to blow themselves up, why nineteen highly educated young men were ready to destroy themselves and thousands of others in the 9/11 hijackings, and why resistance [in Iraq] is growing despite the likelihood of insurgents being killed.[20]

Instead of pausing for contemplation, the governments act – and if thought without action is admittedly ineffective, thoughtless action proves to be equally so, if not worse – and that on top of multiplying the volume of moral corruption and human suffering. As Maurice Druon has pointed out, 'Before launching the war against Iraq, the Americans had only four agents, who moreover proved to be double agents.'[21] Americans started the war assured 'that the American soldiers will be received as liberators, with open arms and bouquets of flowers'. But, to quote from Meacher one more time, 'the death of more than 10,000 civilians, with 20,000 injured and even higher Iraqi military casualties, [was] exacerbated, one year on, by the failure to deliver key public services, . . . rampant unemployment and a gratuitously heavy-handed US military.'

Terrorist forces will hardly budge under military blows. On the contrary, it is precisely from the clumsiness and the extravagant and wasteful prodigality of their adversary that they draw and replenish their strength.

Mark Juergensmeyer has analysed the intricate blend of religion, nationalism and violence in the perpetually simmering and occasionally erupting intertribal hostilities in the Punjab.[22] Focusing particularly on Sikh terrorism, responsible for the deaths of thousands of victims, and among other crimes for the assassination of the Indian Prime Minister Indira Ghandi, he found what he and most other researchers would have expected to find before they embarked on their fieldwork: 'Young rural Sikhs had perfectly good reasons for being unhappy' – the reasons being simultaneously economic, political and social. Their farming produce had to be sold below market prices, their capacity for self-assertion had been reduced virtually to nil by the oppressive policies of the ruling Congress Party, and they felt relentlessly degraded as they fell behind the better-off urban classes. But Juergensmeyer expected also to find evidence of the 'politicization of religion', and for that purpose he studied the teachings of the spiritual leader of the young militant Sikhs, Sant Jarnail Singh Bhindranwale, whom his countless followers worshipped as a saintly martyr. In this case, though, he was surprised. He found only residual and perfunctory references in Bhindranwale speeches to economy, politics or class. Instead, the preacher

[l]ike the legion of Protestant Christian revival speakers that traipsed through the mid-American rural countryside . . . spoke of the struggles between good and evil, truth and falsehood, that reside within each troubled soul, and called for renunciation, dedication, and redemption. It seemed that he was speaking to young men in particular about their easy compromises with the lures of modern life.

More often than in the case of the American Bible Belt preachers, though, one could find in Bhindranwale's sermons references
to contemporary political leaders. Bhindranwale gave his spiritual
war a clearly 'external' dimension: he suggested that the satanic
forces had somehow come down to earth and were now residing
in the official residence of India's head of state . . . Intrigued, Juergensmeyer extended his inquiry to numerous other places, like
Kashmir, Sri Lanka, Iran, Egypt, Palestine, Israeli settlements,
where tribal or class front lines were drawn using religious markers
and where blood was spilled in the name of the hallowed values
of a virtuous, pious and saintly life – and found everywhere
a strikingly similar pattern, not so much of the 'politicization
of religion', as (in his phrase) a *religionization of politics*. Non-
religious grievances, such as issues of social identity and meaningful participation in communal life, once expressed in Marxist or
nationalist vocabularies, tend nowadays to be translated into the
language of religious revival: 'Secular ideological expressions of
rebellion have been replaced by ideological formulations that are
religious. Yet the grievances – the sense of alienation, marginalization, and social frustration – are often much the same.'

Charles Kimball notes a phenomenon akin to the 'religionization of politics' in the vocabulary of the current American administration as well.[23] President Bush, creatively developing the
language introduced into American political life by Ronald
Reagan, is fond of speaking of a 'cosmic dualism' between good
nations, led by the United States, and the forces of evil: 'You had
to align with the forces of good and help root out the forces of
evil.' He is fond of speaking of American military escapades as a
'crusade', and a 'mission' undertaken by Divine commandment.
Henry A. Giroux quotes John Ashcroft, former US attorney
general: 'Unique among nations, America recognized the source
of our character as being godly and eternal, not being civic and
temporal . . . We have no king but Jesus' – and alerts us to the
massive entry of 'moral apparatchiks', politicians who 'believe
that Satan's influence shapes everything from the liberal media to
how Barbra Streisand was taught to sing', on the American political scene.

As the journalist Bill Moyers has written, in this 'Rapture politics',
in which the Bible is read as literally true, dissent is a mark of the

anti-Christ and 'sinners will be condemned to eternal hellfire'. As right-wing religion conjoins with conservative political ideology and corporate power, it not only legitimizes intolerance and anti-democratic forms of political correctness, it also lays the ground-work for a growing authoritarianism that easily derides appeals to reason, dissent, dialogue and secular humanism.[24]

In the infuriatingly multivocal, confused and confusing world of criss-crossing yet mutually incompatible messages whose main purpose may well seem to be the questioning and sapping of each other's reliability, the monotheistic faiths coupled with Mani-chean, black-and-white world visions are about the last fortresses of the 'mono': of *one* truth, *one* way, *one* life formula – of adamant and pugnacious *certainty* and *self-confidence*; the last shelters for the seekers of clarity, purity and freedom from doubt and indecision. They promise the treasures which the rest of the world blatantly and obstinately denies: self-approval, a clear con-science, the comfort of fearing no error and always being in the right. Just like Jamiat Ahli Hadith, a 'strictly orthodox' preacher based in Birmingham, described as practising 'a form of Islam which demands strict separatism from mainstream society. Its website describes the ways of "disbelievers" as "based on sick and deviant views concerning their societies, the universe and their very existence".'[25] Or like Jewish orthodox enclaves in Israel, who, in Uri Avnery's description, have 'their own logic' and 'very little to do with anything else':

> They live in a completely closed, theocratic society that is not influenced by anything happening outside it. They believe in their own world . . . They dress differently and they behave differently. They are a different kind of people all together.
>
> There is very little communication between them and us. They speak a different language. They have a completely different outlook on the world. They are subject to completely different laws and rules . . .
>
> These are people who live separately, in their own communities, religious neighbourhoods, and towns in Israel. They have no contact with ordinary Israeli society.[26]

Indeed, the Manichean vision of the world, the call to arms in a holy war against satanic forces threatening to overwhelm the universe, the reducing of the Pandora's box of economic, political and social conflicts to an apocalyptic vision of a last, life and death confrontation between good and evil: these are not patterns unique to Islamic ayatollahs. On our fast globalizing planet, the 'religionization' of politics, of social grievances and battles of identity and recognition, seems to be a global tendency.

We may be looking in radically different directions and avoid each other's eyes, but we seem to be crowded in the same boat with no reliable compass – and no one steering. Though our rowing is anything but coordinated, we are strikingly alike in one respect: none of us, or almost none, believes (let alone declares) that they are pursuing their own interests – defending privileges already attained or claiming a share in the privileges thus far denied. All sides today seem to be fighting instead for eternal, universal and absolute values. Ironically, we the denizens of the liquid modern section of the globe are nudged and drilled to ignore such values in our daily pursuits and be guided instead by short-term projects and short-lived desires – but even then, or perhaps precisely then, we tend to feel yet more painfully their dearth or absence whenever (if) we try to spot a leading motif in the cacophony, a shape in the fog or a road in the quicksand.

The dangers we fear most are immediate; understandably, we also wish the remedies to be immediate – 'quick fixes', offering relief on the spot, like off-the-shelf painkillers. Though the roots of danger may be straggling and tangled, we wish our defences to be simple and ready to deploy here and now. We resent any solutions that stop short of promising quick effects, easy to achieve, requiring instead a long, perhaps indefinably long time to show results. Even more we resent solutions which require attention to be paid to our own faults and misdeeds, and command us, Socrates-style, to 'know thyself!' And we totally abhor the idea that in this respect there is little if any difference between *us*, the children of light, and *them*, the litter of darkness.

To all such desires and resentments, religions – and particularly *fundamentalist* varieties of *monistic* religions – cater or pander better than any other systems of ideas (with the exception of the totalitarian faiths like communism or fascism – fundamentalist/ monistic religions with modified vocabularies and under different names and management), and certainly much, much better than the non-systemic or even anti-systemic ideas, tentatively voiced, that are resentful of absolutes, as the ideas gestated in staunchly multivocal democracies tend to be. It is as if they were commissioned, customized and tailor-made to satisfy the longings fed by negative globalization, notorious for leaving helms without helmsmen and thereby sapping the credibility of the modern replacement of the omnipotent God with a hopefully self-sufficient humanity. It is as if another 'grand detour' was coming full circle: the modern, swaggering promise that under human management the world would serve human needs better tends to be replaced by a wistful desire for God to repair what the human managers have botched and spoiled.

This current 'replacement of replacement' – the reversal of modern management change, offering a return to the time before the invention of drawing boards – has its advantages. In one go, it reveals the people responsible for one's misery and offers a foolproof way of getting rid of that misery and its culprits. And as long as the pent-up rancour, born of fears that are all the more vexing for being diffuse and of unclear origin, can at long last be released on a tangible target, and right away, it does not matter much that following that way is unlikely to put paid to misery. The recommended strategy cancels the cumbersome task of supplying evidence of the guilt and malice aforethought of the enemies targeted: appointed enemies can't prove their innocence, since their guilt lies in having been authoritatively accused, not deriving from what they do or intend to do, but from what they are. They are – as everyone around will confirm – hereditary (and that means inborn, genetically determined, unredeemable) sinners, heathens, infidels, tools of Satan, dark forces standing between present corruption and that cosy, homely and safe dreamworld purified of their poisonous, carcinogenic presence.

All that would probably have its application to the patent office rejected – were the present-day fundamentalist preachers claiming 'intellectual property rights'. What they offer to their would-be converts is only an openly and blatantly desecularized version of the totalitarian temptations that accompanied the whole of modern history, being tested with particular zeal and to most spectacular effect by the communist and fascist movements of the century that has just drawn to its close.

Tzvetan Todorov offers an in-depth analysis of that temptation at work while pondering on the reminiscences of Margarete Buber-Neumann,[27] a remarkable witness of both the main varieties of the twentieth century's totalitarian horror. She was lured to join the communist ranks in the early 1920s together with many thousands of other young and well-educated men and women, similarly bewildered and appalled by the inanities and inhumanity of a society torn apart and thrown out of joint by the senseless butchery of the Great War, and like her searching in vain for a meaningful life in an apparently meaningless world. The moment she took the decision to join the ranks, Margarete acquired a community of like-minded people, thousands of 'brothers' and 'sisters' sharing their thoughts, fate and hopes; she 'belonged' now, she was freed from the harrowing experience of loneliness among the lonely, she had turned into a part of a powerful whole – 'the word WE was written all over in very large letters,' she remembers. 'Suddenly,' Margarete adds, 'everything appeared to me wondrously easy to understand.' Was that clarity the effect of rubbing shoulders with so many others 'like her', marching in step and elbow to elbow along the only right, noble and ennobling, road? Almost a century later, PR people of our times would suggest exactly such an explanation, repeating as they do on every occasion that 'so many happy customers can't be wrong!'

Todorov comments that when people join ranks, they acquire at long last the certainty they craved and find a response to every question – instead of drifting amidst hesitations, fretting in the grip of doubt. Companionship and certainty (are they not synonyms?!) are what are promised by the siren songs sung by the recruiting officers of the militantly religious or pugnaciously secular camps of the 'great simplification': a life free from doubt, and absolution from the vexing and harrowing necessity of making choices and taking responsibility.

Muslims are not the only people prone to listen to and keen to be seduced by siren voices. And if they do listen and surrender to seduction, they don't do that because they are Muslims; being Muslims only explains why they prefer the voice of mullahs or ayatollahs to the voices of sirens of other denominations. Others, who listen as keenly and allow themselves to be seduced as gladly without being Muslims, will be offered a rich assortment of other siren songs, and will no doubt find tunes among them they will easily recognize as comfortingly familiar and resonant with their own.

It so happens, though, at the start of the twenty-first century, that for many young Muslims being a Muslim means being a victim of multiple deprivation, as well as being cut off from (or barred from using) the public escape routes leading out of oppression, along with the paths of personal emancipation and the pursuit of happiness which so many other, non-Muslim men seem to tread with such astonishing, and aggravating, facility.

Young Muslims have reason to feel that way. They belong to a population officially classified as lagging behind the 'advanced', 'developed', 'progressive' rest of humanity; and they are locked in that unenviable plight through collusion between their own ruthless, high-handed governments and the governments of the 'advanced' part of the planet, ruthlessly turning them away from the promised and passionately coveted lands of happiness and dignity. The choice between the two varieties of cruel fate, or rather two parts of that fate's cruelty, feels like choosing between the devil and the deep blue sea. The young Muslims try to cheat, smuggle or force their way around the 'swirling swords and Cherubs' guarding the entrance to the modern paradise, only to find (if they manage to cheat the guards or glide past the check points) that they are not welcome there, that they are not allowed to catch up with the very way of life they are accused of and ridiculed for not chasing after keenly enough; and that being there does not mean sharing in the sort of happiness and dignified life which drew them in.

They are indeed in a double bind: rejected by their community of origin for desertion and treachery, and barred entry by the community of their dreams because of alleged incompleteness and insincerity, or worse still because of the perfection and ostensible blamelessness of their betrayal/conversion. Cognitive dissonance, always a harrowing and painful experience of an intrinsically irrational plight that does not allow for a rational solution, is in their case doubled. Their reality denies the values they were groomed to respect and cherish, at the same time as it refuses them the chance of embracing the values they are being insistently exhorted and enticed to embrace – even if the messages encouraging them to embrace those values are notoriously confused and confusing (Integrate! Integrate! But woe to you if you try, and damnation if you succeed . . .) Shame and vengeance on both your houses . . . (Let's note that among the victims of the Islamic terrorists of the last few years the numbers of 'brother (and sister, and infant) Muslims' by far exceeded the numbers of all the others. Since Satan and his henchmen/tools are not choosy, why should his detractors and would-be conquerors be?)

What renders the opacity (the ambivalence, the irrationality) of such a plight yet deeper is that the Muslim world itself, by a geopolitical coincidence, seems to be placed across a barricade. It so happens that the economy of the rich, 'advanced' countries is grounded in extraordinarily high oil consumption (dependent not just on the petrol destined to be burned up in car engines, but also on oil-derived raw materials for essential industries), while the economy of the US, by far the largest military power, thrives thanks to petrol prices being kept artificially low. It also happens that the most profuse supplies of crude oil, and the only ones promising to remain economically viable by the middle of the century, are under the administration of Islamic (more exactly, Arab) governments. Arabs hold their fingers on the lifelines of the West – the main taps from which the life-giving energy of the opulent and powerful West flows. They may – just may – cut its supply, with virtually unimaginable, but certainly dramatic (catastrophic from the point of view of Western powers) consequences for the planetary balance of power.

The havoc another catastrophe (a 'natural' one, Katrina) played with the capacity to act and the preservation of law and order in the most powerful of those powers may be seen as a preliminary rehearsal of what may happen if the Arab governments, the nominal owners of the largest reserves of oil on the planet, do succeed in tightening their grip on the oil taps. This is what the *New York Times* correspondent Jad Mouawad saw in the aftermath of winds blowing at a speed of 175 miles per hour, throwing out of action offshore platforms and onshore wells that had been supplying more than a quarter of American domestic oil production, and forcing into idleness 10 per cent of the country's refining industry:

> Drivers waiting in line for hours, and occasionally in vain, to fill
> up their tanks. The president urging everyone to curtail driving

and conserve energy at home. Dark rumours of hoarding and market manipulation starting to spread. Economists warning that soaring energy costs will certainly slow economic growth – and maybe snuff it out completely . . .

Says Vincent Lauerman, the global energy analyst at the Canadian Energy Research Institute: 'What we have right now is a runaway freight train. There's nothing I can see between it and higher prices' . . .

'We are in uncharted territory,' said John Felmy, the chief economist at the American Petroleum Institute, the industry's main trade group . . .

Robert Mabro, president of the Oxford Institute for Energy studies . . . added: 'If people can't get gas, they become furious, they become violent, they create trouble. Energy is a necessity.'[28]

'Energy markets', Mouawad concludes, 'are at the mercy of the slightest glitch anywhere around the globe that can push the prices even higher.' And 'if oil hit 100 dollars' per barrel, it would, in the opinion of William Hunter, another expert analyst, 'have quite a debilitating effect' on airlines and the whole transportation sector, and the economy as a whole 'would slow down to a crawl'. Let's note however that even if the effort to arrest the runaway growth of oil prices brings the hoped-for results, the relief may be only temporary; and with China, India and Brazil joining the car-driven economies, and with the planetary supplies of oil grinding slowly yet relentlessly close to exhaustion, also very short-lived. Already in the year and a half *preceding* the Katrina disaster, the price of crude oil on the New York exchange doubled (from 33 to 66 dollars a barrel). And the pace of growth of the annual demand for fuel doubled as well.

This concatenation of circumstances has two effects, both adding to the apparently incurable ambiguity of the Muslims' plight.

The predictably acute interest of the 'modern part' of the planet in securing exclusive control over the most precious supplies of crude oil casts them into direct confrontation with a large part of the Islamic world. Since the apocryphal meeting of Franklin D. Roosevelt with King Saud on board an American cruiser, when the American President guaranteed to keep the Saudi dynasty in power over the almost empty yet fabulously oil-rich peninsula, whereas the newly appointed king promised an uninterrupted

supply of oil to be pumped by American companies, and since the
CIA arranged a putsch to topple the democratically elected Mos-
sadeq government in Iran half a century ago, Western countries,
and the US in particular, have not been able to stop interfering in
the Middle Eastern Islamic regimes, intermittently using lavish
bribes, threats of economic sanctions or direct military interven-
tion as their primary weapons. They have also, on the sole condition of keeping the oil taps open and the petrol pipelines full,
helped to keep in power reactionary (and in the case of the
Wahabi-dominated Saudi kingdom radically fundamentalist)
regimes that had clearly passed their use-by and tolerate-until
dates and in all probability wouldn't have been able to hold their
own if it hadn't been for the Western, mainly American, military
umbrella.

It was through the services of its special envoy Donald Rumsfeld, now Defense Secretary, that the US promised to support
Saddam Hussein's dictatorship in Iraq with billions of dollars of
agricultural credits and millions of dollars worth of cutting-edge
military technology, as well as satellite intelligence that could be
used to direct chemical weapons against Iran – and kept their
promise. Kings and dictators at the helm of such regimes are keen
to use their good fortune to surround themselves with the most
whimsical toys Western consumer society can offer, while strength-
ening their border guards and arming their secret police against
smuggling in the products of Western democracy. Fleets of cars
full of gadgets yes, free elections no; yes to air conditioning, but
no to the legal equality of women; and the most emphatic 'no' to
an equitable distribution of sudden riches, to personal freedoms
and to political rights for subjects.

The *hoi polloi* given a chance to taste Western imports at first
hand are therefore most unlikely to develop a profound liking for
the fruits of Western civilization. The siren tunes sung by the
mullahs, wary of the secular inclinations of liberal democracy, are
certain to find numerous keen listeners not only among the great
and mighty who share in their anti-Western resentment for fear
of democratic threats to their privileges, but also among the millions of their subjects bypassed in the distribution of imported
comforts. Some of the latter would be willing to die so that the
comfortable life of the former may continue. And most of the
former would gladly set aside a fraction of their fabulous riches

so that the latter could be trained to do just that and volunteer to use their skills in practice.

Another effect of the peculiar concatenation of circumstances is apparently the opposite: the selectively 'Westernized' section of the elite in the rich Islamic countries can stop wallowing in their inferiority complex. Thanks to their 'nuisance power', their potential control over riches which the West needs but does not possess, they can feel strong enough to attempt the final step: to claim a status superior to those who so blatantly depend for their survival on the resources which they, and they only, can claim to command. Nothing is so reassuring about one's might as the fact of being bribed by the mighty . . .

The calculation could hardly be simpler or more obvious: if only *we* gain undivided control over the fuel which feeds their engines, *their* juggernaut will grind to a halt. *They* will need to eat from *our* hands and play the game according to the rules *we* set. The strategy, however, unlike the calculation of chances, is neither simple nor self-evident. Though *we* have enough means to buy more and more weapons, all the bribe money that finances buying them won't be enough to get equal with *their* military power. The alternative, even if only a second best, is to deploy another weapon of which *we* possess as much, if not more, than *they* do: our nuisance potential, the power to make the power struggle too costly to continue, not worth continuing or downright impossible to continue. Considering the blatant vulnerability of their homelands, their kinds of societies, the destructive capacity of our nuisance power may well transcend the admittedly awesome potential of their massive weapons. It takes, after all, much less stuff and men and labour to bring a city like New York or London into a state of paralysis than to smoke out a single terrorist commander from his mountain cave or to chase his subalterns out of the cellars and attics of urban slums . . .

When all textbook as well as other, home-made or cottage industry remedies for cognitive dissonance have been tried, and they have all stopped short of reaching the hoped-for result, the only thing left is the agonisingly pathetic condition of laboratory rats who have learned that savouring the titbits piled up at the far end of the maze can be enjoyed only along with the horrors of electric shocks. Perhaps escaping the maze once and for all (an option not open to laboratory rats) will bring the satisfaction which the most diligent learning and mapping of the twists and turns of its many corridors never will?

Whether those trapped do or don't try to find an exit from the oppression – and whether they do or don't go on hoping without hope that the escape route from the dissonance may be found on their own side of the maze's walls – does not seem to make much difference to their plight. Prizes for obedience are tantalizingly slow to come, while penalties are visited daily for not trying hard enough or trying too hard (and what could the trying *not* 'too hard' possibly be like if it is not going to be immediately condemned as 'not hard *enough*'?!).

Becoming a terrorist is a choice; allowing oneself to be blinded by sheer jealousy, resentment or hatred is also a choice. Being penalized for confronting, genuinely or putatively, such choices is not however a matter of choice since that confrontation is the verdict of fate. The fact that a few people 'like you' made the wrong choices is enough to deprive you of the right to make your own – right – choice; and if you have made it nevertheless, that same fact will prevent you from convincing those who sit in judgment, or usurp the right to pass verdicts, that you've made it – and made it sincerely.

A few suicidal murderers on the loose will be quite enough to recycle thousands of innocents into the 'usual suspects'. In no time, a few iniquitous individual choices will be reprocessed into the attributes of a 'category'; a category easily recognizable by, for instance, suspiciously dark skin or a suspiciously bulky rucksack – the kind of object which CCTV cameras are designed to note and passers-by are told to be vigilant about. And passers-by are keen to oblige. Since the terrorist atrocities on the London Underground, the volume of incidents classified as 'racist attacks' rose sharply around the country. In most cases not even the sight of a rucksack was needed to provoke it.

A dozen or so Islamic plotters, ready to kill, proved to be enough to create the atmosphere of a besieged fortress and raise a wave of 'generalized insecurity'. Insecure people tend to seek feverishly for a target on which to unload their gathering anxiety, and to restore their lost self-confidence by placating that offensive, frightening and humiliating sentiment of helplessness. The besieged fortresses into which the multi-ethnic and multicultural cities are turning are habitations shared by both the terrorists and their victims. Each side adds to the fear, passion, fervour and obduracy of the other. Each side confirms the worst fears of the other and adds substance to their prejudices and hatreds. Between themselves, locked into a sort of liquid modern version of the *dance macabre*, the two sides won't allow the phantom of a siege ever to rest.

In his study of the surveillance technology introduced on a massive scale into the streets of cities after September 11, David Lyon notes its 'unintended consequences': 'a widening of the surveillance web . . . and an enhanced exposure to monitoring of ordinary people in their everyday lives'.[29] We can argue however that among all its 'unintended consequences' pride of place belongs to surveillance technology's 'media is the message' effect. Specialized, as it is bound to be, in seeing and recording external, visible and recordable objects, that technology is also bound to be oblivious to the individual motives and choices behind the recorded images, and so must lead eventually to the substitution of the idea of 'suspicious categories' in place of individual evildoers. As Lyon puts it,

> The culture of control will colonize more areas of life, with our permission or without, because of the understandable desire for security, combined with the pressure to adopt particular kinds of systems. Ordinary inhabitants of urban spaces, citizens, workers, and consumers – that is, people with no terrorist ambitions whatsoever – will find that their life-chances are more circumscribed by the categories in which they fall. For some, those categories are particularly prejudicial, restricting them from consumer choices because of credit ratings, or, more insidiously, relegating them to second-class status because of their colour or ethnic background. It is an old story in high-tech guise.

The anonymous detective who apologized to Girma Belay, the hapless Ethiopian refugee and marine engineer, after the police brutally entered his London flat, stripped him naked, punched him, pinned him to the wall, arrested him and held him for six days without charge, by saying 'Sorry mate – wrong place, wrong time',[30] could (and should) have added: 'and wrong *category*'. And this is how Belay sums up the consequences of that categorial, even if individually suffered experience: 'I am in fear; I don't want to go out.' And he blames his plight on those 'bastard terrorists' who 'acted in such a way that all sweetness and freedom was destroyed for people *like me*' (italics added).

In a vicious loop, the threat of terrorism turns itself into an inspiration for more terrorism, spilling on its way ever greater volumes of terror and ever larger masses of terrorized people – the two products which terrorist acts, deriving their name from precisely such an intention, are bent on producing and plot to produce. One may say that the people who are terrorized are the terrorists' most reliable, even though unwilling, allies. The 'understandable desire for security', always ready and waiting to be played on by a crafty and astute exploiter, and now whipped up by scattered and apparently unforeseeable acts of terror, proves in the end to be the main resource on which the terror may count to gather momentum.

Even in the unlikely event that the borders were sealed against undesirable flesh-and-bone travellers, the likelihood of another terrorist outrage would not be reduced to nil. Globally generated grievances float in global space as easily as finance and the latest fashion in music or clothes, and so too does the urge to take revenge on their genuine or putative culprits or (if the culprits are inaccessible) the most suitable and handy scapegoats. Wherever they land, global problems settle down as local, quickly striking roots and becoming 'domesticated' – and having found no global resolution, they seek local targets on which to unload their resulting frustration. Escaping arrest, Hussain Osman, one of the main suspects in the London Underground bombing, arrived in Italy, though according to Carlo De Stefano, a top official of the Italian anti-terror policy, no links were found between him and any local terrorist group there – 'he did not appear to be in contact with any known terrorist groups'. 'It seems we are seeing an impromptu group acting alone in this case,' Stefano concluded.[31]

The injuries inflicted by the powers veering out of control on the negatively globalized planet are countless and ubiquitous – and above all scattered and diffuse. In all parts of the planet, the soil for the seeds of terrorism is well prepared and the travelling 'masterminds' of terrorist outrages can reasonably hope to find some fertile plots wherever they stop. They don't even need to design, build and maintain a tight structure of command. There are no terrorist armies, only terrorist *swarms*, synchronized rather than coordinated, with little or no supervision, and only ad hoc platoon commanders or corporals. More often than not, for a 'task group' to be born apparently *ab nihilo* it will suffice to set a properly spectacular example and leave it to be obligingly and promptly disseminated and hammered into millions of homes by the constantly spectacle-hungry TV networks through all the information highways along which they set their messages moving.

Never before has the old anthropological notion of 'stimulus diffusion' (meaning the prototypes and inspirations which travel across lands and cultures without, or independently of, their original practitioners or mediators and without their 'natural habitat', the forms of life in which they were born and have grown) grasped so well the character of present-day cross-cultural communication and the contagious, epidemic potential of cultural innovations. On a planet criss-crossed by information highways, the messages will find and select their own grateful listeners without even seeking them out; or rather they will be infallibly found and selected by their potential and grateful listeners who will gladly take the chore of searching ('surfing the web') upon themselves.

The meeting between messages and listeners is greatly facilitated on a planet turned into a mosaic of ethnic and religious diasporas. On such a planet, the past separation between the 'inside' and the 'outside', or for this matter between the 'centre' and 'periphery', is no longer tenable. The 'externality' of life-threatening terrorism is as notional as is the 'internality' of life-sustaining capital. Foreign-born words become flesh inside the country of arrival; alleged 'outsiders' prove in most cases to be locally born and bred individuals inspired/converted by ideas *sans frontières*. There are no front lines – only separate, widely dispersed and eminently mobile battlefields; no regular troops – only civilians turning soldiers for a day and soldiers on indefinite civilian leave. Terrorist 'armies' are all *home* armies, needing no barracks, no rallies and no parade grounds.

The machinery of the nation-state, invented and groomed to guard territorial sovereignty and to set insiders unambiguously apart from outsiders, has been caught unprepared by the 'wiring up' of the planet. Day after day, one terrorist atrocity after another, the state-run law-and-order institutions learn of their own ineptitude to handle the new dangers which have blatantly put paid to

the orthodox, hallowed and ostensibly tested and reliable categories and distinctions.

The ad hoc responses of those institutions to successive surprises betray confusion. A day after the pugnacious Islamist
preacher Sheikh Omar Bakri, probably fearing being faced with
incitement charges, left Britain for Lebanon (allegedly for a
holiday), leading politicians on both sides of the party-political
divide called for strict control of the country's own residents going
out (thus far a custom associated primarily with the totalitarian
states of yore) just as foreigners wishing to enter have been thus
far controlled. Two days later John Prescott, the Deputy Prime
Minister, advised Bakri publicly: 'Enjoy your holiday, make it a
long one' – probably wishing that by running away Bakri had
indulged the state authorities, getting them out of the awkward
predicament in which they would have been placed by an unprecedented move to revoke Bakir's indefinite leave to stay in the
country: 'Although the home secretary, Charles Clarke, cannot
stop Mr Bakri coming back under existing legislation, he would
be able to block his entry under the plans announced last Friday
to exclude or deport those who preach hate or justify violence.'[32]
A quandary, indeed, with no good solution; or perhaps rather an
illusionary dilemma, reflecting solely the strategic and tactical
confusion of the state authorities? By leaving the country, Bakri
escaped justice, and the fact that he could do it with impunity is
not the best of testimonies to the British security services; but –
paradoxically – the intention is to redefine justice as the right to
force culprits to leave and to bar them from returning . . .

The plight of a 'stranger', cast and held in a disturbingly under-
defined 'grey zone' stretching between declared enemies and
trusted friends, has been at all times ambivalence incarnate.
Modern states have tried hard to eliminate or at least reduce that
ambivalence, harrowing for those cast in the category of strangers,
but also causing a lot of discomfort to those who cast them there.
It was perhaps from pondering the convoluted (and inconclusive)
story of such efforts that Carl Schmitt's famous/infamous definition of sovereignty as the 'right to exempt' was coined.

At a less theoretical level, passports and visas, residence rights
and their refusals, naturalization and its refusal – all meant to end
the ambiguity if not of *social*, then at least of *legal* status – deserve
to be counted among the most notable of modern inventions.

Negative globalization and its offshoots (the unprecedented degree of extraterritoriality of capital, trade, information, crime and terrorism) have, however, made all such tested instruments of sovereignty by and large ineffective. The prospect that the sovereign right to exempt will ensure victory in the war declared on the ambivalence affecting strangers, or at least guarantee an upper hand in successive battles, now looks in no way certain; the twin-edged sword of inclusion/exclusion proves to be too blunt to secure victory or even keep hope of it alive. To hit two birds with one stone – to retain an ability to act in a new world of diasporas and the tangle of 'external' and 'internal' connections and clashing loyalties which can no longer be untied and held apart, while still preserving space for manoeuvre when faced with rapidly changing situations in the future – the powers that be seem to be veering towards making an *ambivalence* of legal status, rather than an *unambiguity* of residence and civil rights, 'indefinite'.

All that does not promise an early freedom from ambivalence, that profuse source of anxiety, insecurity and fear suffered in equal measure by people caught in it and people living their lives in their obtrusive presence. No quick fix is conceivable, let alone at hand. With the increasingly diasporic spread of the world's populations and with the orthodox hierarchy of cultures all but dismantled, any suggestion of a replacement is likely to be hotly contested. With the very notions of cultural superiority and inferiority eliminated from the 'politically correct' vocabulary, such a traditional way – once universally tested – of fixing and solidifying the outcomes of successive resolutions of ambivalence as 'cultural assimilation' (now politely renamed 'integration', while remaining loyal to the past strategy) is neither acceptable nor any longer likely to be adopted and followed through to the end.

Having leaked from a society forcefully opened up by the pressure of negative globalization forces, power and politics drift ever further in mutually opposite directions. The problem that will in all probability confront the current century as its paramount challenge is to bring power and politics together again; whereas the task likely to dominate the current century's agenda is to find a way of performing such a feat.

The reunion of the separated partners inside the domicile of the nation-state is perhaps the least promising of the possible responses to the challenge. On a negatively globalized planet, all the most fundamental problems – the genuinely *meta*-problems which condition the chances and the ways of tackling all other problems – are *global*, and being global they admit of no *local* solutions.

There are no local solutions to globally originated and globally invigorated problems, and there cannot be. The reunion of power and politics will have to be achieved, if at all, at the planetary level. As Benjamin R. Barber poignantly put it, 'no American child can feel safe in its bed if children in Karachi or Baghdad don't feel safe in theirs. Europeans won't be able to boast for long about their freedoms if people in other parts of the world remain deprived and humiliated.'[33] Democracy and freedom can no longer be assured in just one country or even in a group of countries; their defence in a world saturated with injustice and inhabited by billions of human beings denied human dignity will inevitably corrupt the very values it is meant to protect. The future of democracy and freedom has to be made secure on a planetary scale – or not at all.

Fear is arguably the most sinister of the many demons that nest in the open societies of our time. But it is the insecurity of the present and uncertainty about the future that hatch and breed the most awesome and least bearable of our fears. The insecurity and uncertainty, in their turn, are born of a sense of impotence: we seem no longer to be in control, whether singly, severally or collectively, of the affairs of our communities, just as we are not in control of the affairs of the planet – and we become increasingly aware that we are unlikely to be free of the first handicap as long as the second is allowed to persist. To make our situation still worse, we lack the tools that could allow our politics to be lifted to the level where power has already settled, so enabling us to recapture and repossess control over the forces shaping our shared condition, and thereby to define the range of our options as well as draw limits to our freedom to choose: the kind of control which has presently slipped out – or has been torn out – of our hands.

The demon of fear won't be exorcised until we find (or more precisely *construct*) such tools.

5

Setting Fears Afloat

The paradox rightly pointed out by Robert Castel in his incisive analysis of the profuse fears, born of and fed by insecurity, that saturate liquid modern life is that 'we – at least in the developed countries – live undoubtedly in some of the most secure [*sûres*] societies that ever existed'.[1]

We, men and women living in the 'developed' part of the world (that is the world's richest, most modernized and still most keenly modernizing part), are 'objectively' the most secure people in the history of humanity. As statistics amply demonstrate, the dangers threatening to shorten our lives are fewer and further between than they used to be in the past and than they are in other parts of the planet; and we have exceptionally ingenious and effective means to anticipate, prevent and fight back against those dangers that could still make us die early or fall ill. All the objective measures conceivable show an apparently unstoppable rise in the protection which men and women of the 'developed' part of the globe enjoy on all the three fronts where the battles in defence of human life are fought: against the superior forces of nature, against the inborn weaknesses of our bodies, and against the dangers emanating from the aggression of other people.

And yet it has been precisely in that unprecedentedly secure and comfortable part of the world – in Europe and its former dominions, overseas offshoots, branches and sedimentations, as well as in a few other 'developed countries' with a European connection of elective affinity, a relationship of a *Wahlverwandschaft* rather than *Verwandschaft* kind – that the addiction to fear and the securitarian obsession have made the most spectacular careers in the recent years. Contrary to the objective evidence, it is the people who live in the greatest comfort on record, more cosseted and pampered than any other people in history, who feel more threatened, insecure and frightened, more inclined to panic, and more passionate about everything related to security and safety than people in most other societies past and present.

The modern promise to avert or defeat all the threats to human security one by one has been to some extent fulfilled – though not the arguably exaggerated, overly ambitious and in all probability unfulfillable promise of doing away with them altogether. What however has blatantly failed to materialize is the expectation of freedom from the *fears* born of and fed by insecurity.

Trying to explain that mystery, Castel suggests that our acute feeling of insecurity derives not so much from the dearth of protection as from the inescapable 'unclarity of its scope' (*ombre portée*) in the kind of social universe that, like ours, 'has been organized around the endless pursuit of protection and a frantic search for security'[2] – thus setting ever rising, previously unthinkable standards of protection, always ahead of what it is currently possible to achieve. It is our 'security obsession', and our intolerance of any minor – even the tiniest – breach in security provision which it prompts, that becomes the most prolific, self-replenishing and probably inexhaustible source of our anxiety and fear.

We can guess that the bane of our harrowing experience of insecurity, which shows no sign of abating and is apparently incurable, is that side-effect of, so to speak, 'rising expectations'; the uniquely modern promise and the widespread conviction it has spawned that, given continuing scientific discovery and technological invention, the right skills and proper effort, 'full' security, a life completely free from fear, can be achieved – that 'it can be done', and 'we can do it'. The lingering anxieties stubbornly suggest however that the promise has not been met – that 'it has *not* been done'. When this is combined with the conviction that it *could* be, this frustration of hopes adds the insult of impotence to the injury of insecurity – and channels anxiety into a desire to locate and punish the culprits, as well as get indemnity/compensation for the hopes that have been betrayed.

In two of the three areas which gave birth to the insecurities haunting men and women of premodern times (the eminently extravagant and intractable powers of nature, and the vexing frailty of the human body), spectacular developments occurred throughout the modern era. A protective technological shield was put between the caprices of nature and our own habitat, moving some way towards a comfortable homeostatic regularity of the latter – though suspicions are growing, played down by some experts but voiced ever more loudly by many others, that the price we will need to pay for that (transient) success may be an unprecedented, growing and perhaps no longer resistible destructiveness of the natural elements. As to the second area – more bodily ailments or even inborn faults have been made curable than ever before, and even if the sum total of illnesses and their victims shows no sign of subsiding, and even if our ever recurring suspicions as to the healthiness of our diet may be well founded, the statistical longevity of our lives keeps steadily growing.

As to the third area however – that of the interhuman enmities and ill will – it is almost unanimously agreed that the promised security did not just fail to materialize in full, but did not come any closer, and might even have drifted farther away. The degree of self-assurance and feelings of safety have abominably failed to grow, as we seem to move from one 'safety panic' to another, each panic no less if not more frightening than the one before. Since the successive outbursts of safety panic usually follow the news that some human institutions (hospitals, prisons and parole services, food factories and supermarkets, water purification plants, etc.) are less than foolproof and don't function as smoothly as one had assumed (and was encouraged to believe), the fears that result tend to be explained by wicked deeds with evil intent. Of this sort of drama, there must be a villain – a human villain. And as we've seen before (in chapter 2), it is also humans – *other* humans, of course, cruel or selfish but either way callous and unlike us – that in expert opinion and popular beliefs alike bear a large part of the responsibility for the pranks of nature and the vagaries of bodily health.

We can say that the modern variety of insecurity is marked by a fear mostly of *human* maleficence and of *human* malefactors. It is shot through by the suspicion of evil motives on the part of certain specific men and women, or of specific groups or categories of men and women; and often also by a refusal to trust the constancy, dedication and reliability of human companions, a refusal that is almost inevitably followed by our unwillingness to make companionship solid, durable and thus trustworthy.

Castel charges modern individualization with the foremost responsibility for such a state of affairs. He suggests that having substituted an individual duty of self-concern, self-interest, self-love and self-care (*l'amour propre* instead of *l'amour de soi*, to use Jean-Jacques Rousseau's memorable distinction) for the closely knit communities and corporations that once defined the rules of protection and their related individual rights and obligations, and monitored their observance, modern society was built on the quicksand of contingency. Exhorted, nudged and pressed daily to pursue their own interests and satisfactions, and to concern themselves with the interests and satisfactions of others only so far as they affect their own, modern individuals believe other individuals around them to be guided by similarly egotistic motives – and so cannot expect from them any more disinterested compassion and solidarity than they themselves are advised, trained and willing to offer. In such a society, the perception of human company as a source of existential insecurity and as a territory strewn with traps and ambushes tends to become endemic. In a vicious circle of sorts, it exacerbates in its turn the chronic frailty of human bonds and adds further to the fears which that frailty is prone to gestate.

Once visited upon the world of humans, fear becomes self-propelling and self-intensifying; it acquires its own momentum and developmental logic and needs little attention and hardly any additional input to spread and grow – unstoppably. In David L. Altheide's words, it is not fear of danger

> that is most critical, but rather what this fear can expand into, what it can become . . . Social life changes when people live behind walls, hire guards, drive armoured vehicles . . . carry mace and handguns, and take martial arts classes. The problem is that these activities reaffirm and help produce a sense of disorder that our actions perpetuate.[3]

Fears prompt us to take defensive action, and taking defensive action gives immediacy, tangibility and credibility to the genuine or putative threats from which the fears are presumed to emanate. It is our response to anxiety that recasts sombre premonition as daily reality, giving a flesh-and-blood body to a spectre. Fear takes root in our motives and purposes, settles in our actions and saturates our daily routines; if it hardly needs any further stimuli from outside, it is because the actions it prompts day in, day out supply all the motivation, all the justification and all the energy required to keep it alive, branching out and blossoming. Among the mechanisms that claim to follow the dream of perpetual motion, the self-reproduction of the tangle of fear and fear-inspired actions seems to hold pride of place . . .

Though this is, of course, an illusion – just as it always was in the case of innumerable other *perpetuum mobile* mechanisms claiming the miracle of energy self-sufficiency. The cycle of fear and fear-dictated actions would not roll on uninterrupted and go on gathering speed were it not drawing its energy from *existential tremors*.

The presence of such tremors is not exactly news. Existential tremors have accompanied humans through the whole of their history, with none of the social settings in which human life-pursuits used to be conducted offering foolproof insurance against the 'blows of fate' ('fate': an expression coined to set apart unforeseeable and unpreventable misfortunes from those adversities that *could* be anticipated and averted). The idea of 'fate' implies not so much the peculiar nature of the blows it brings as the *human inability* to predict them, let alone prevent or tame them; it implies the helplessness and haplessness of the victims, rather than the particular cruelty of the damage and loss. 'Fate' stands out from other disasters by striking without warning and by its blindness to what its victims do or abstain from doing in order to escape its blows. 'Fate' has always stood for human ignorance and impotence, and owed its awesomely frightening power to the resourcelessness of its victims.

Perhaps the sole distinction of the present-day fears is the *decoupling* of fear-inspired actions from the existential tremors that generated the fears that inspired them; the *displacement* of fears, from the cracks and fissures in human defences where 'fate' is hatched and incubated, to the areas of life largely *irrelevant* to the genuine source of anxiety but instead – consolingly – within sight and reach. The snag is, of course, that no amount of effort invested in the areas into which the fears have been displaced is likely to neutralize or block their genuine sources, and so it is bound to prove impotent to placate the original anxiety, however earnest and ingenious the effort might be. It is for this reason that the vicious cycle of fear and fear-inspired actions (ostensibly preventive or defensive) rolls on, losing none of its vigour – yet coming no nearer to its end.

The cycle in question has been displaced in the present time from the sphere of security (that is, of self-confidence and self-assurance, or their absence) to that of safety (that is, of shelter from, or exposure to, threats to one's own person and its extensions). The first sphere, progressively stripped of institutional state-supported and state-insured scaffoldings, has been opened up to the vagaries of the market and turned into a playground of the global forces operating in the 'space of flows' stretching beyond the reach of political control, and so also beyond the ability of their victims (already affected by their actions or fearing to be affected soon) to respond adequately, let alone to resist effectively. Communally endorsed insurance policies against individual misfortune, which in the course of the last century came to be known collectively under the name of the 'social' ('welfare') state, are now being phased out, reduced below the level needed to validate and sustain confidence in security, or are no longer hoped, let alone trusted, to survive the next round of cuts.

In a summary of the most recent trends, Neal Lawson observes that the government 'becomes merely the hand-maiden for the global economy'.[4] No longer is the state the omnipotent master of its territory – neither really nor putatively, neither in its practice nor in its dreams, neither in its current work nor in its boldest ambitions. Lawson agrees with Thomas Frank in his diagnosis of the rise and rise of 'market populism', 'with the market now viewed as the ultimate tool of democracy' and 'each individual "casting their vote" all day everyday for the good and services that matter to them'.[5] 'Everywhere the collective voice . . . is replaced by atomised and competitive individualised choices.'

Handmaiden of global economic powers or not, the state cannot simply send in a letter of resignation (to what address?!), pack up its belongings and absent itself. It remains in charge of law and order inside its territory and goes on being held responsible for the way this function is performed. Paradoxically, it is precisely its meek and ever fuller surrender to other powers, both inside and outside its territory but in each case beyond its control, that makes well-nigh inescapable not just the retention but the expansion, extensive as well as intensive, of its order-protecting, policing function. 'By freeing the market still further and allowing its boundaries to seep into the public sector, the government has to pick up the bills of market failure, of externalities the market refuses to recognise, and act as a safety net for the inevitable losers of market forces.'[6]

Let us note however that it is not just the occasional market *failures* that prompt the present shift in governmental priorities. The deregulation of market forces and the surrender of the state to one-sidedly 'negative' globalization (that is, globalization of business, crime or terrorism, but not of political and juridical institutions able to control them) needs to be paid for, and *daily*, in the currency of social disruption and devastation: in that of the unprecedented frailty of human bonds, the ephemerality of communal loyalties and the brittleness and revocability of commitments and solidarities – whose consequences saddle state governments with no less a burden than did the tasks related to the establishment, maintenance and daily servicing of the social state. It is a day in, day out *normality*, not the occasional failures of deregulated markets and negative globalization, that now prompts the growth, ever faster, of the social bills which governments find themselves obliged to pick up.

As the protective network of social rights weakens and is no longer trusted to last for the time needed to offer a solid frame for future plans, the bane of insecurity and fear, which the vision of the social state had proposed to eliminate once and for all, returns; but it is now obliged to seek other remedies, elsewhere. To quote Lawson once more: 'As there is nothing else to fall back on it is likely that people then give up on the whole notion of collectivism . . . and fall back on the market as the arbiter of provision.' And markets, notoriously, act at cross-purposes with the intentions of the social state. The market thrives under conditions of insecurity; it capitalizes on human fears and feelings of haplessness.

With state-maintained defences against existential tremors progressively dismantled, and arrangements for collective self-defence, such as trade unions and other instruments for collective bargaining, following suit under the pressure of a competitive market that erodes the solidarity of the weak, it is left now to individuals to seek, find and practise individual solutions to socially produced troubles – and to do all that by individual, singly undertaken and solitary actions, equipped with individually possessed and operated tools and resources that are blatantly inadequate to the task. Offering more flexibility as the sole remedy for an already unbearable volume of insecurity, the messages coming from the sites of political power paint the prospects of yet more challenges and greater privatization of troubles – and so ultimately more, not less, uncertainty. They leave little hope of collectively assured existential security, and instead encourage their listeners to focus on their individual safety in an increasingly uncertain and unpredictable, and so potentially dangerous, world.

Ubiquitous care 'from the cradle to the grave' could be felt to be oppressive, sometimes infuriatingly so. Compared with as yet untested, and so even more tempting varieties of market commodities, it might seem dull, insipid and drab, lacking 'spice', stripped of that modicum of change, surprise and challenge which life needs to steer clear of unsavoury and incapacitating boredom. This kind of care, of which the classic 'social state' now stands accused, was castigated for being excessive; it invited widespread rebellion.

In tune with the public mood, Margaret Thatcher famously launched and conducted her frontal assault against the 'nanny state' under the slogan 'I want the doctor of my choice at a time of my choice'. As a programme, this struck a responsive chord when it was announced. Choice seemed indeed to be a welcome relief from routine. The surprises and challenges that choice brought in its wake were soon found however to exude a disturbing, often unbearable volume of uncertainty. The road leading to the right choice of doctor and the right timing for a visit proved, to be sure, less tediously monotonous than before, but it was found instead to be strewn with stumbling blocks and pitfalls of an unfamiliar, but no less alarming and annoying variety. Having explored the waiting rooms of hospitals and doctors' surgeries and spoken to a great number of patients anxiously waiting their turn, Jan Hoffman for instance found out that 'within the past decade, the shift in the doctor–patient conversation – from 'This is wrong with you, here's what to do', to 'Here are your options, what do you want to do? – became all but complete. Baby boomers had gotten what they had asked for. And then some . . .'[7]

Hoffman goes on to quote opinions voiced by bewildered patients:

> It's like being in a foreign country; you don't speak the language, and you're trying to find directions . . .

> When a doctor says, 'Here are your options', without offering expert help and judgment, that is a form of abandonment . . .

> You want to know who is managing your health care? It's you or no one . . .

To find yourself 'abandoned' 'in a foreign country', unsure of direction and knowing that 'no one' will help you to avoid a blunder and share responsibility for its consequences, is – everybody will tell you – a frightening experience. Freedom with no security feels no less dreadful and off-putting than security without freedom. Both conditions are menacing and pregnant with fear – the alternatives of the devil and the deep blue sea.

The difference between now and then is that by now both situations have been tried – experienced in the lifespan of one generation; and both have been found wanting. What we know now but could be ignorant of before is that in whatever respects the two situations might differ from one another, the power to generate fear is not one of them. Fear is perhaps deeper now and more frightening, since there seems to be no escape; at least not a kind of escape that seems credible – in spite of the zealous search for a 'third way'. Most obviously, it is not obvious at all what individuals – to whom the task falls of individually finding individual solutions to a socially produced quandary, and then deploying individual resources to put them into practice – might do to free themselves from their fears, let alone to avoid being haunted by them in the first place.

Admittedly, the example I used to illustrate this plight was derived from a situation in which the individuals felt particularly vulnerable and for this reason it is painted in particularly lurid colours. The issue under discussion is not however confined to health and health care; neither can the blame for the quandary with 'no good solution' be laid at the door of medicine (not only medicine, at any rate). Similar troubles and worries await individuals (infallible choosers by decree, foreigners in a foreign country by fate) wherever and whenever their knowledge and skills are inadequate to tackle the world's complexity, inept at vouching for the wisdom of their choices, and sorely insufficient to control their own predicament; and that means always, and everywhere. In a moment of reflection (if such a moment can be found and spared amidst the perpetual, time-consuming bustle) they may ponder, and agree with, Woody Allen's description of their dilemma: 'More than at any other time in history, mankind faces a crossroads. One path leads to despair and utter hopelessness. The other, to total extinction. Let us pray we have the wisdom to choose correctly . . .'[8]

As the editors of the *Hedgehog Review* wrote in the introduction to their special issue dedicated to fear, 'in the absence of existential comfort' people tend to settle 'for safety, or the pretence of safety'.[9]

The English word 'safety' (absent, by the way, from many other European languages) mostly evokes the *personal* – material, bodily – aspects of security, and so the above quotation suggests that people tend to settle for the *security of their bodies and their extensions*: homes and their contents, streets through which bodies move, vulnerable and defenceless as they appear to be to blows that are particularly frightening and painful for being sudden and unexpected. But since it is the absence of 'existential security' (or the absence of confidence in its duration) that triggers the whole process, the safety concerns people 'settle for' are not the genuine cause of the troubles that prompt their feverish search for that settlement.

The current settlement means that in the first (in practice the only) place it is from the realm of *safety* that one wishes and struggles these days to eliminate 'fate'. It is in that realm that one fights for control, full control and continuous control – hoping against hope to own, or acquire, enough skills and resources to attain it, and so that the task will eventually prove to be realistic and sooner or later repay the effort invested. As a result, the other realms oozing and spreading fear remain unattended. All hope of controlling them is abandoned; and rightly so, since as long as the task is undertaken individually, those realms are indeed bound to stay uncontrollable.

The snag is that the actions that promise to be effective tend by and large to be irrelevant to the true causes of anxiety – whereas the potentially relevant actions stay stubbornly ineffective. After all, the most acute of the 'existential tremors' sapping confidence and breeding the torments of uncertainty are hatched in an area unreachable by the tools at the disposal of individuals and so we are doomed to find them uncontrollable. The ground on which our life prospects rest is admittedly shaky and friable – as are our jobs and the companies that offer them, our partners and networks of friends, the standing we enjoy in wider society and the self-esteem and self-confidence that come with it.

'Progress', once the most extreme manifestation of radical optimism and a promise of lasting happiness universally shared, is fast turning into its opposite, drifting towards the dystopian and fatalistic pole of our anticipations. The idea of 'progress' now stands mostly for the threat of relentless and inescapable change, but change surmised rather than predicted with any degree of certainty (or for that matter amenable to such a prediction), let alone planned. Instead of auguring peace and respite, future changes portend continuous strain without a moment of rest, threatening to posit new and unfamiliar demands and invalidate the hard-learned routines of coping. The image of 'progress' is turning into a likeness of an endless game of musical chairs in which one moment of inattention will result in irreversible defeat and irrevocable exclusion; or into a version of *The Weakest Link* played for real. With the real significance of each successive 'step forward' being, as in that tele-reality show, the eviction and bankruptcy of the person who was the slowest in taking it. Instead of great expectations and sweet dreams, 'progress' evokes sleepless nights filled with the nightmares of being left behind – of missing a train, falling out of the window of a fast-accelerating vehicle, of no longer being up to the task, or being assessed as such by others who caught up with the changed circumstances more swiftly. Exclusion is, after all, the *waste* of progress; and one wonders whether it is indeed its sideline, or rather its main line of production and staple product: its latent, yet genuinely principal function . . .

There are yet more reasons to be afraid. One of them can be located in the deficit of normative regulation. With no authority

daring or/and potent enough to claim universality for the norms
it prefers and wishes to promote, and no authority able to ensure
the binding potency of its preferred and promoted norms, the
rules guiding human interaction are thrown back into the melting
pot as soon as they are suggested. It is now left largely to individuals to negotiate on their own what are admittedly *provisional* and
local settlements to their disagreements. Even if agreed and temporarily obeyed by all involved, the settlements cannot be trusted
to last; their hold on their signatories (not to mention those who
refused to sign) is weak and uneven, and everyone involved needs
an uninterrupted vigilance – lest the other protagonists retreat
from their commitment with little or no warning. All commitments are 'until further notice' – and it is unclear who is entitled
to give such notice, let alone under what circumstances and for
what reason. In the absence of clear guidelines, one can assume
that a succession of trials and errors, though notorious for its risks
and traps, is the second best choice. Just to stay where you are
and hold on to the place you have reached, you need to run, and
run, and run. You are pressed and cajoled and nudged and nagged
to keep on the move, or else . . . Otherwise you'll find yourself
overtaken and left behind.

The lightning speed of fashion changes is but one – boringly
obvious, banal – example: the moment you have made your carefully calculated identity-and-aspiration statement by meticulously
dovetailing all the elements of your public appearance, from hair-
style to shoes and 'accessories', the elements drop or reverse their
meanings: meanings fall away faster than the time it takes to
articulate and absorb them. The whirls of fashions swallow and
devour everything around. You thought, for instance, that you'd
finally composed your ideal home, put all the finishing touches to
it, paid off the credit card debts which putting them all together
required, and that now you could sit down, enjoy the view and
pride yourself on having arrived? Well, think again. 'Here today,
gone tomorrow,' muses Caroline Roux, *Guardian* expert and
truly knowledgeable adviser on home/design/property.

> Wrong as it may be, interiors are becoming as prone to the blink-
> and-miss-it turnarounds as the world of fashion . . .
>
> The latest item to be put on the superannuated list is the chan-
> delier. I know. I'm sorry. Especially after all the trouble you went
> to . . .

Wooden blinds, wooden floors: don't expect them to last forever, at least not in credibility terms. Consumer durables they are no longer.[10]

Go and rip up the floor then, and the windows, and . . . Are there any 'consumer durables' left? 'Consumer durable': has it not become an oxymoron, a contradiction in terms?

Writing at the heyday of the 'solid' phase of modernity and developing Basil Bernstein's memorable distinction between 'restricted' and 'elaborated' codes, Mary Douglas suggested that whereas the child in working-class families 'is controlled by the continual building up of a sense of social pattern', having its question 'why must I do it?' answered regularly with curt reminders of the patterns irrevocably ascribed to a place in a hierarchy of power ('because I say so'), gender ('because you are a boy'), seniority ('because you are the oldest'), etc., in middle-class families 'control is effected through either the verbal manipulation of feelings or through the establishment of reasons which link the child to his acts'.[11] Douglas concluded that 'in this way the child is freed from a system of rigid positions, but made a prisoner of a system of feelings and abstract principles'. Writing in the 1960s, Douglas could believe that the two codes were simply alternative instruments of *effective* control, and that they were such instruments thanks to the ability of both of them to credibly appeal to something *stable*, rigid, intractable and unquestionable – the social structure in the first case, abstract principles in the other.

The middle classes, let's comment, never had the (doubtful) luxury of referring to the kind of hard-and-fast necessities which only a rigid social structure might frame. After all, the *middle* classes derived their name from being placed 'betwixt and between': in the *middle*, and for that reason ambiguous, ground – stretched between the two 'magnetic poles' of two polar social categories. Being so placed, they always faced a degree of 'underdetermination' unknown to other classes, as well as a constant challenge to reconfirm their standing – a kind of challenge which members of other classes did not face (there is pretty little aristocrats *need* to do to keep their identity, while the lower classes *can* do next to nothing to change it; it is only the middle classes who *must* work hard to remain what they are). Though structurally underdetermined, the middle classes could in the past nevertheless deploy as a weapon an invocation of something else equally solid and binding: solid *rules* called 'principles' – and treat this invocation as an effective instrument of control. Neither of the two 'solid' alternatives to which reference was made at the time Mary Douglas wrote *Natural Symbols* can, however, now be presumed to be as solid and as widely (whether gladly or resentfully) adopted as they were at the height of the solid modern era.

Few people nowadays would be ready to claim for their own, *personal* choices the kind of irresistible authority that once emanated from the *socially* enforced order – and if they did make such a claim, there would be only a meagre chance that their authority would be accepted and obeyed. The social settings for the life pursuits of contemporary men and women are now more reminiscent of a scene of perpetual war, with innumerable reconnaissance sorties and battles being staged and fought daily; battles that tend to be aimed not so much at the promotion of a consistent and durable code of behaviour – let alone at promoting a code bidding for universal acceptance – as at testing the limits (if any) of allowable and realistic individual choice, and assessing the extent of the ground to be gained within or outside those limits. Once the deficit of legitimacy becomes the feature of all bids and claims, the actions undertaken in their name and for their sake, once upon a time perceived as the only proper expressions of the immutable, uncontestable and irresistible order of things, tend to be recast in the public view as acts of enforcement and so of *violence*; that is, as specimens of *il*legitimate coercion. A widespread impression of a fast-rising volume of violence results: another prolific source of contemporary fears.

Fears of this kind are scattered and diffused over the whole spectrum of life pursuits. Their sources stay hidden and stoutly resist mapping; the mystery in which those sources are wrapped further magnifies their fear-inspiring potential. If only we could focus our apprehensions, and the actions intended to mitigate the pain they cause, on an object that can be easily and unambiguously located and so will be, hopefully, possible to deal with and therefore, at least in principle, amenable to control! As long as fears resist being focused like this, we are doomed to grope in the dark. Perhaps staying close to better-lit places is a less harrowing choice, even if it proves pointless in the end.

Aggravated by our inability to slow down the mind-boggling pace of change, let alone to predict or determine its direction, we tend to focus on things we can, or believe we can, or are assured that we can, influence. We try to calculate and minimize the risk of falling victim to those dangers that are easiest to locate, the most pliant and tractable, among all the uncounted and uncountable dangers we suspect the opaque world and its uncertain future to hold in store. We are engrossed in spying out 'the seven signs of cancer' or 'the five symptoms of depression', or in exorcising the spectre of high blood pressure and a high cholesterol level, stress or obesity. In other words, we seek *substitute* targets on which to unload the surplus existential fear that has been cut off from its natural outlet, and find makeshift targets in taking elaborate precautions against inhaling someone else's cigarette smoke, ingesting fatty foods or 'bad' bacteria (while avidly swilling liquids promising to contain the 'good' ones), exposure to the sun, or unprotected sex. Those of us who can afford it fortify themselves against visible or invisible, present or anticipated, known or still unfamiliar, scattered yet ubiquitous dangers through detoxifying the insides of our bodies and our homes, locking ourselves behind walls, surrounding the approaches to our living quarters with TV cameras, hiring armed guards, driving armoured vehicles or taking martial arts classes.

'The problem', however, to recall David L. Altheide's warning, 'is that these activities reaffirm and help produce a sense of disorder that our actions precipitate.' Each extra lock on the entry door in response to successive rumours of foreign-looking criminals wrapped in cloaks bulging with daggers, or every overhaul of our diet in response to another 'food panic', makes the world look *more* treacherous and fearsome, and prompts still *more* defensive actions that will add still *more* vigour to the self-propagating capacity of fear.

A lot of commercial capital can be garnered from insecurity and fear; and it is. 'Advertisers', comments Stephen Graham, for instance, 'have been deliberately exploiting widespread fears of catastrophic terrorism, to further increase sales of highly profitable SUVs.'[12] The gas-guzzling quasi-military monsters grossly misnamed 'sport utility vehicles' that at some point reached 45 per cent of all car sales in the US are being enrolled into urban daily life as 'defensive capsules'. The SUV is

a signifier of safety that, like the gated communities into which
they so often drive, is portrayed in advertisements as being immune
to the risky and unpredictable urban life outside . . . Such vehicles
seem to assuage the fear that the urban middle classes feel when
moving – or queuing in traffic – in their 'homeland' city.

Eduardo Mendietta is yet more pungent in his analysis of the
message the sudden American love for SUVs (or 'Hummers')
conveys:

Before the Hummer had been popularized, we already had the
image of a vehicle that would be uniquely armoured and outfitted
to engage the jungles of concrete and urban mayhem – this was
the armoured car of the battlefield. The Hummer . . . simply capitalizes on an already produced need: the need to be prepared to
move through the burning city, the collapsing city of post-sixties
urban unrest . . . [The SUV is] assuming and insinuating, not too
covertly, that the city is a battlefield and jungle to be both conquered and escaped.[13]

The SUV is just one example of the commercial uses to which
fears may be put, as long as they remain 'decoupled' from their
sources, set afloat, diffused, underdefined and unfocused; many
people will pay an arm and a leg for the comfort of knowing what
they ought to be afraid of, and for the satisfaction of having done
all that can be done to act on that knowledge. Like liquid cash
ready for any kind of investment, the capital of fear can be turned
to any kind of profit – commercial or *political*. And it is.

Whereas personal safety has become a major, perhaps even *the*
major selling point in the marketing strategies of consumer commodities, the guardianship of 'law and order', increasingly nar-
rowed down to the promise of personal safety, has become a
major, perhaps *the* major selling point in political manifestoes and
electoral campaigns alike – while displays of threats to personal
safety have been promoted to the rank of a major, perhaps *the*
major asset in the mass media ratings war, adding yet more to the
success of both the commercial and the political uses of fear. (As
Ray Surette puts it, the world as seen on TV resembles 'citizen-
sheep' being protected from 'wolves-criminals' by 'sheepdogs
– police'.)[14]

There are, indeed, many ways to capitalize on the growing supplies of free-floating, unanchored and unfocused fears; for instance, gaining political legitimacy and approval by flexing government muscles in declaring war on crime and more generally on 'disturbances of public order' (a wide, and in liquid modern settings probably bottomless category, able to accommodate the whole range of uncomfortable 'others' – from the homeless sleeping rough to truants from school).

Loïc Wacquant has recently suggested that 'the securitarian merry-go-round is for criminality what pornography is to love relations',[15] because it totally ignores the causes and meaning of its ostensible object and reduces its treatment to taking 'positions' selected solely by the virtue of their being spectacular; and because it is put on public display not for its own sake but for the sake of publicity. Public display condenses attention on 'recidivists, obtrusive beggars, refugees on the move, immigrants to be expelled, prostitutes on sidewalks and other kinds of social rejects who litter the streets of metropolises to the displeasure of the "decent people". For that purpose, the battle against crime is staged as a "titillating bureaucratic-mediatic spectacle".'

It would be inane or insane to deny the reality of crime and crime-related dangers. The point is, though, that the weight of crime among other public concerns tends to be measured, as does the weight of all other objects of public attention, by the extensiveness and intensity of the publicity it is accorded, rather than by its innate qualities. Joseph Epstein's vivid portrayal of the phenomenon of 'celebrity' similarly captures the most conspicuous aspects of the fascination with safety – that, so to speak, generic 'negative celebrity' of the liquid modern era. 'Much modern celebrity', Epstein suggests, 'seems the result of careful promotion'; celebrity is based 'on broadcasting' of an achievement, but also on 'inventing something that, if not scrutinized too closely, might pass for achievement'. And he concludes: 'Many of our current-day celebrities float upon "hype" which is really a publicist's gas used to pump up and set floating something that doesn't quite exist.'[16] One is also reminded of Ulrich Beck's similar comments on the characteristics of contemporary risks: as most contemporary dangers are inaccessible to personal scrutiny and cannot be reliably confirmed or disproved with the means personally possessed, they can be argued as easily 'into' public beliefs as 'out' of them. And in the battle of opinions those with the strongest broadcasting muscle stand the best chance of winning.

The new individualism, the fading of human bonds and the wilting of solidarity, are all engraved on one side of a coin whose other side bears the stamp of globalization. In its present, purely negative form, globalization is a parasitic and predatory process, feeding on the potency sucked out of the bodies of nation-states and other protective contraptions which their subjects once enjoyed (and occasionally suffered) in the past. In Jacques Attali's view, the nations organized into states now 'forfeit their influence on the general run of affairs and abandon to globalization all means of directing the destiny of the world and of resisting the many forms that fears may assume'. Or, as Richard Rorty points out,

> The central fact of globalization is that the economic situation of the citizens of nation states has passed beyond the control of the laws of that state . . . We now have a global overclass which makes all the major economic decisions, and makes them in entire independence of the legislatures and *a fortiori* of the will of the voters of any given country . . . The absence of a global polity means that the super-rich can operate without any thought of any interests save their own. We are in danger of winding up with only two genuinely global, genuinely international, social groups: the super-rich and the intellectuals, that is, the people who attend international conferences devoted to measuring the harms being done by their super-rich fellow cosmopolitans.[17]

Rorty could add a third 'social group' to the list of cosmopolitans, comprising drug traffickers, terrorists and other criminals of all, save the humblest and relatively least threatening, kinds.

And he could as well qualify his description of the intellectualist branch of the cosmopolitans. Quite a few of them attend conferences intended to praise the glory of the new 'global overclass' instead of attempting to measure the harms they have done and are doing. They follow closely (and sometimes precede, as trailblazers) the global itinerary of the 'super-rich'. They are usually referred to under the generic name of 'neoliberals'. The message and the practices they strive to make global are known under the name of 'neoliberalism' – an ideology aspiring to become, in Pierre Bourdieu's memorable warning, *la pensée unique* of the inhabitants of the planet Earth. Neoliberalism, to borrow John Dunn's poignant phrase, is a 'wager on the strong' – 'a wager on the rich, to some degree perforce on those with the good fortune of being rich already, but above all on those with the skill, nerve and luck to make themselves so'.[18] Neoliberals, in Lawrence Grossberg's summary of their ideology,

> tend to believe that, since the free market is the most rational and democratic system of choice, every domain of human life should be open to the forces of the marketplace. At the very least, that means that the government should stop providing services that would be better delivered by opening them up to the marketplace (including presumably various social service and welfare provisions) . . .
>
> Finally neoliberals are radical individualists. Any appeal to larger groups . . . or to society itself, is not only meaningless but also a step towards socialism and totalitarianism.[19]

Such ideological blackmail helps negative globalization run smoothly. Few political leaders are bold enough or sufficiently resourceful to stand up to the pressure – and if they do, they must reckon with formidable adversaries: an alliance between the two branches of the 'global overclass' – extraterritorial capital and its neoliberal acolytes. Save for a few (notably Nordic) exceptions, most politicians select the easy option: TINA – the 'there is no alternative' formula. And yet, as Polly Toynbee has recently reminded us, 'People are left to presume that there is no alternative to some malign economic force beyond human control. The truth is that penury and greed are political choices, not economic destiny; we can be Nordic, not American, and we can be John Lewis, not Gate Gourmet, employers if we choose.'[20]

Whatever the codicils that could be added to Rorty's verdict quoted above, his main message is incontestable. Indeed, society is no longer adequately protected by the state; it is now exposed to the rapacity of forces the state does not control and no longer hopes or intends to recapture and subdue – not singly, not even in combination with several other similarly hapless states.

It is mainly for that reason that state governments, struggling day in, day out to weather the storms threatening to play havoc with their programmes and policies, stumble from one ad hoc crisis-management campaign and one set of emergency measures to another, dreaming of nothing more than staying in power beyond the next election, and otherwise devoid of far-sighted programmes or ambitions – not to mention visions of a radical resolution to the nation's recurrent problems. 'Open' and increasingly defenceless on both sides, the nation-state loses a good deal of its might, now evaporating into global space, and a lot of its political acumen and dexterity, now increasingly relegated (or dumped?) into the sphere of individual 'life politics', and (as the current political jargon has it) 'subsidiarized' to individual men and women. Whatever remains of past might and politics in the charge of the state and its organs gradually dwindles to a volume that is perhaps sufficient to furnish a large-size police precinct equipped with cutting-edge surveillance technology – and that is about all. The reduced state can hardly manage to be anything more than a *personal safety state*.

The retreat of the state from the function on which for a better part of the past century its most persuasive claims to legitimation were founded has thrown the issue of its political legitimation wide open again. A citizenship consensus ('constitutional patriotism', to deploy Jürgen Habermas' term) cannot presently be built, as it promised to be not so long ago, on assurances of protection against the vagaries of the market, notorious for sending tremors through people of whatever social standing and threatening everybody's rights to social esteem and personal dignity.

Under such circumstances, an alternative legitimation of state authority and another formula for the benefits of dutiful citizenship need urgently to be found; unsurprisingly, it is currently being sought in protection against dangers to *personal safety*. In the political formula of the personal safety state, the spectre of an uncertain future and social degradation against which the then *social* state swore to insure its citizens not so long ago is being gradually yet consistently replaced by the threat of a paedophile let loose, a serial killer, an obtrusive beggar, mugger, stalker, prowler, poisoner of water and food, terrorist: or better yet by all such threats rolled into one in the virtually interchangeable figures of the native 'underclass' or the illegal immigrant, a foreign body from birth to death and forever a potential 'enemy within', against whom the security state promises to defend its subjects tooth and nail.

In October 2004 a documentary series was broadcast by BBC2 under the title *The Power of Nightmares: The Rise of the Politics of Fear.*[21] Adam Curtis, the writer and the producer of the series and an acclaimed maker of serious television programmes in Britain, pointed out that though global terrorism is an all-too-real danger continually reproduced inside the 'no man's land' of the global wilderness, a good deal if not most of its officially estimated threat 'is a fantasy that has been exaggerated and distorted by politicians. It is a dark illusion that has spread unquestioned through governments around the world, the security services, and the international media.' It wouldn't be too difficult to trace the reasons for the rapid and spectacular career of this particular illusion: 'In an age when all the grand ideas have lost credibility, fear of a phantom enemy is all the politicians have left to maintain their power.'

Numerous signals of the imminent shift in legitimation by state power to that of the personal safety state could be spotted well before 11 September – even if people needed, it appears, the shock of the falling towers in Manhattan to be reproduced in slow motion and for months on end on millions of TV screens for the news to sink in and be absorbed, and for politicians to reharness the popular existential anxieties to a new political formula. It was not mere coincidence that (according to Hugues Lagrange) the most spectacular 'safety panics' and the loudest alarms about rising criminality – coupled with ostentatiously tough responses from governments and manifested among other ways in rapidly rising prison populations ('substitution of a prison state for the social state', in Lagrange's phrase) – have occurred since the mid 1960s in countries with the least developed social services (like Spain, Portugal or Greece) and in countries where social provision had started to be drastically reduced (like the United States and Great Britain).[22] No research conducted up to the year 2000 showed any correlation between the severity of penal policy and the volume of criminal offences, though most studies did discover a strong (negative) correlation between 'incarceration push' on the one hand and 'the proportion of market-independent social provision' and 'the part of the GNP earmarked for that purpose' on the other. All in all, the new focus on crime and on dangers threatening the bodily safety of individuals and their property has been shown beyond reasonable doubt to be intimately related to the rising 'sentiment of [social] vulnerability', and to follow closely the pace of economic deregulation and of the related substitution of individual self-reliance for social solidarity.

Excess does not mark explicitly anti-terrorist operations alone; it is salient as well in the alerts and warnings the anti-terrorist coalition address to their own populations. As Deborah Orr observed a year ago, many flights were intercepted yet were never found to have been actually under threat. 'The tanks and troops were stationed outside Heathrow, even though they eventually withdrew without finding anything at all.'[23] Or take the case of the 'ricin factory', the discovery of which was publicly and vociferously announced in 2003: it was 'trumpeted as "powerful evidence of the continued terrorist threat", although in the end the germ warfare factory at Porton Down couldn't prove that any ricin had ever been in the flat touted as a significant terrorist base'. And, finally, 'although 500 people [up to the beginning of February 2004] have been held under the new terrorist laws, only two have been convicted' (and let us note: however minuscule that proportion is, it is still infinitely higher than that of the prisoners convicted among the inmates of Guantanamo after several years of imprisonment without charge).

Though the British Home Secretary Charles Clarke is obviously right when he warns that it is 'absolutely foolish' to assume that there will not be another terrorist attack in London, the measures undertaken by the government to counter the threat of terrorism look as if they had been calculated to deepen still further the mood of emergency and entrench a 'besieged fortress' complex, rather than to cut down the likelihood of another terrorist atrocity. As suggested by Richard Norton-Taylor, the *Guardian* security editor, 'there is a real danger that the prime minister's 12-point outbursts' – the announcement of new arrest-and-deportation measures against terrorist suspects, measures grossly bypassing the established judiciary procedure – 'will be counterproductive, alienating the very people that the government – and not least [the security and intelligence] agencies – need on their side'.[24]

Deborah Orr points out that in the light of all such inanities the hypothesis of powerful trade interests being instrumental in fanning the terrorist scare must be accorded at least some credibility. Indeed, there are indications that the 'war on terror', instead of combating the worldwide proliferation of trade in small weapons, has increased it considerably (and the authors of a joint report by Amnesty International and Oxfam aver that small weapons are 'the real weapons of mass destruction', since half a million people are killed by them each year).[25] The profits drawn by American producers and traders of 'self-defense stuff and gadgets' from the popular fears which in turn are magnified by the very ubiquity and high visibility of such stuff and gadgets have been amply documented. All the same, it needs to be repeated that the staple and the most massive product of the war waged against the terrorists accused of sowing fear has so far been the fear itself.

The other prolific side-product of that war are the new limits imposed on personal freedoms – some of them unheard of since the time of the Magna Charta. Conor Gearty, Professor of Human Rights Law at the London School of Economics, has listed a long inventory of laws limiting human liberties which have already been passed in Britain under the rubric of 'anti-terrorist legislation', and agrees with the opinion of numerous other worried commentators that it is by no means certain whether 'our civil liberties will still be here when we seek to pass them on to our children'.[26] The British judiciary has so far, with only a few (if keenly publicized) exceptions, complied with the governmental policy that 'there is no alternative to repression' – and so, as Gearty concludes, 'only liberal idealists' and other similarly deluded well-wishers 'expect the judicial branch to lead society' in the defence of civil liberties in this 'time of crisis'.

As I write these words, there has not as yet been any judicial response in Britain to the 'shoot to kill' tactics adopted by the Metropolitan Police; the tactics which in their first application led to the death of Jean Charles de Menezes, whose only guilt was to have been (falsely) identified by the police as a prospective suicide bomber and who, contrary to (false) explanations after the fact, was unaware of being followed, never ran from the police and did not jump over the ticket barrier. Indeed, one does need nowadays to be wary of the threat of more terrorist outrages. But one needs as well to eye with suspicion the guardians of order that might (mis)take oneself for a carrier of that threat . . .

The stories about the dark exploits inside the camp at Guantanamo or Abu Ghraib prison, cut off not only from visitors but from the reach of any law, whether national or international, and of the slow but relentless descent into inhumanity of men and women appointed to supervise that lawlessness, have been publicized in the press widely enough to save us from repeating them here.[27] It is necessary however to point out that the atrocities disclosed and publicized were neither isolated incidents nor 'accidents at work'. According to all we have learned *ex post facto* (though we still cannot swear that we know the whole story), they were carefully designed and their executors were diligently trained in the state-of-the-art skills the job required. Modern science and its highly placed spokesmen were brought in to update the techniques of torture:

> Military doctors at Guantanamo Bay, Cuba, have aided interrogators in conducting and refining coercive interrogations of detainees, including providing advice on how to increase stress levels and exploit fears . . . The program was explicitly designed to increase fear and distress among the detainees . . . The military refused to give *The [New York] Times* permission to interview medical personnel at the isolated Guantanamo camp . . . The handful of former interrogators who spoke to *The Times* about the practices at Guantanamo spoke on condition of anonymity; some said they had welcomed the doctors' help.[28]

General Ricardo S. Sanchez, 'the former American commander in Iraq during the Abu Ghraib prison abuse scandal', was promoted by Defense Secretary Donald H. Rumsfeld to a new senior position in the army command. As the *New York Times* reporters comment, the promotion 'seems to reflect a growing confidence that the military has put the abuse scandal behind it'.[29]

'There are no terrifying new monsters. It's drawing the poison of the fear', observed Adam Curtis.[30] Fears are there, saturating daily human existence as the deregulation of the globe reaches deep into its foundations and the defensive bastions of civil society fall apart. Fears are there, and drawing on their apparently inexhaustible and self-reproducing supplies in order to rebuild depleted political capital is a temptation many a politician finds it difficult to resist.

Well before 11 September, surrender to that temptation, complete with its redoubtable benefits, was already well rehearsed and tested. In a study poignantly and aptly named 'The Terrorist, Friend of state Power', Victor Grotowicz analysed the uses to which the government of the German Federal Republic put the terrorist outrages perpetrated by the Red Army Faction at a time when the 'glorious thirty years' of the social state began to show the first signs of drawing to a close.[31] He found that whereas in 1976 only 7 per cent of German citizens considered personal safety to be a paramount political issue, two years later the considerable majority of Germans viewed it as much more important than the fight against rising unemployment and galloping inflation. During those two years the nation watched on their TV screens the photo-opportune exploits of the rapidly swelling forces of the police and secret service, and listened to the ever bolder auction bids of their politicians as they tried to outwit each other in promising ever tougher and more severe measures to be deployed in the all-out war against the terrorists.

Grotowicz found as well that, while the liberal spirit inspiring the original emphasis of the German constitution on individual freedoms had been surreptitiously replaced with the state authoritarianism previously so resented, and while Helmut Schmidt publicly thanked the lawyers for refraining from testing in court the new Bundestag resolutions against the constitutional law, the new legislation played mostly into the hands of the terrorists, enhancing their public visibility (and so obliquely their social stature) well beyond the levels they could conceivably have reached on their own. According to the shared conclusion of the researchers, the violent reactions of the forces of law and order added enormously to the popularity of the terrorists. One has to suspect that the manifest function of the stern new policies, declared to be the eradication of the terrorist threat, was playing second fiddle to their latent function, which was the effort to shift the grounds of state authority from areas which the state neither could nor dared or intended to effectively control, to another area – where its powers and determination to act could be spectacularly demonstrated, to public applause.

The most evident result of that anti-terrorist campaign was a rapid increase in the volume of fear saturating German society. As for the terrorists, the campaign's declared target, it brought them closer to their own target, to sap democracy-sustaining values, than they could otherwise have dreamt of. The final irony was that the eventual falling apart of the Red Army Faction, and its disappearance from German life, was not brought about by repressive police action; it was due to changed social conditions, no longer fertile to the terrorists *Weltanschauung* and practices.

Much the same can be said of the sad story of Northern Irish terrorism, obviously kept alive and, at some point, growing in popular support owing in large measure to the harsh military response of the British; its end can be ascribed more to the Irish economic miracle and to a psychological phenomenon akin to 'metal fatigue' than to anything the British army contingents maintained in Northern Ireland for so many years undertook to do, or did, or were capable of doing.

The personal safety state, the latest replacement for the ailing social state, is not known for being particularly democracy friendly; most certainly not as intensely and devotedly so as the social state it intends to replace.

Democracy draws on the capital of people's trust in the future and sanguine self-confidence in their ability to act, and the social state was historically instrumental in bringing such confidence to the parts of society for which that confidence had remained off-limits for the greater part of history; the social state made self-confidence, and trust in the accessibility of a better future, the common property of all the state's citizens. The personal safety state, on the contrary, draws on fear and uncertainty, the two arch-enemies of confidence and trust, and like any institution it develops vested interests in multiplying the sources of its nourishment as well as in colonizing new, heretofore virgin lands that can be converted into its plantations. Obliquely, it saps thereby the foundations of democracy.

Just as the crisis of citizens' self-confidence and trust signals hard times for democracy, falling levels of fear might sound a death knell for a state seeking its legitimation in the defence of threatened law and order. The rise of the personal safety state may well portend the approaching twilight of modern democracy. It may also prove to be instrumental in recycling that foreboding into a self-fulfilling prophecy.

'Security states' are not necessarily totalitarian; in some of its crucial aspects, the personal safety state, their liquid modern variety, even appears the direct opposite of the totalitarian state.

In Tzvetan Todorov's apt summary of its constitutive attributes, totalitarianism consists in a *soi-disant* 'unification' of the totality of individual life.[32] In a fully fledged totalitarian state the boundaries between the public and the private are blurred and tend to be effaced altogether, and the initiatives of the state are no longer limited by the unencroachable individual liberties of its citizens, deemed sacrosanct. (Cornelius Castoriadis would say that the *ecclesia* invades, conquers and colonizes the *oikos*, annexing the *agora* on its way.)[33] But this is clearly not the tendency dominant in the liquid modern state. On the contrary, ever larger chunks of the public sphere that was once administered and managed directly by state organs tend to 'trickle down': be 'subsidiarized', 'contracted out', 'hived off' to private institutions, or simply vacated by state-run agencies and abandoned to the care and responsibility of individuals. It looks as if the *oikos* is now on the offensive, while *ecclesia* is in retreat.

The state is no longer bent on replacing spontaneity with routine, contingency with charts and schedules, and more generally 'chaos' (that is, the self-assertion and competition of autonomous agents) with order (that is, the rearranging, but above all the reducing of the range of probable outcomes) – all those earlier ambitions which (as Hannah Arendt noted) fed and kept on the rise its endemic and ubiquitous totalitarian tendency. In this respect at least, the tendency of the state under liquid modern conditions runs in exactly the opposite direction. In another respect, however, a clear 'totalitarian slant' can indeed be spotted.

According to Mikhail Bakhtin, the 'constitutive moment' of all earthly powers is 'violence, suppression, falsehood' and the 'trepidation and fear of the subjected'.[34] Writing from beneath one of the two thickest and most oppressive sediments of the last century's totalitarian tendency (communist and nazi), Bakhtin was inclined to unpack the intimate connection between the dominion of the state and the 'trepidation and fear of the subjected' as primarily, or even exclusively, the subjects' fear *of* the state, oozing from the perpetual practice and even more constant threat of the state's violence.

This was indeed the distinctive mark of the twentieth century's totalitarian regimes, which obtained and maintained the submission and obedience of its subjects by means of state-promoted terror. That terror arose from the randomness, whimsicality and apparent absence of logic in the way in which totalitarian states practised the exemption from law – otherwise a universal (and defining, according to Carl Schmitt) prerogative of all sovereign powers. The totalitarian state was feared as the *source of the unknown and the unpredictable*: as the perpetual, irremovable element of uncertainty in the existential condition of its subjects. (This, to be sure, applied to the communist variant of totalitarian regime to a much greater extent than to the nazi; having disposed of free market competition, another major source of existential anxiety, and exempted most life processes from the destabilizing and uncontrollable interference of *economic* forces, the communist regime had to rely on deliberately *manufactured* uncertainty, an *artificial* insecurity produced by *political* means, that is by overt and ubiquitous coercion.) Todorov quotes Ernest Renan's third *Dialogue philosophique*, a half-forgotten bizarre *plaidoyer* for totalitarian practices, suggesting that the state needs to replace the 'chimerical hell' of the netherworld, used by religions to frighten the faithful into obedience but whose existence could not be convincingly proved to the living, with an earthly, all-too-real, tangible sort, certain to be waiting for everyone straying from the right path.[35]

Even in communist regimes, however, the state powers strove to present themselves to their oppressed subjects as *saviours* from terror, rather than its primary *source*. Once state terror became the norm, any momentary respite in the course of a successive 'purge', the revocation of any sentence and any personal exemption from wholesale persecution were to be received as another testimony of the state's benevolence, and of the earnestness of the state efforts to protect the innocent and reward the obedient – and so as one more confirmation that the resolve to vest one's trust in the state as the sole island of logic and consistency amidst a sea of anarchy and contingency was the right decision to take.

The 'trepidation and fear of the subjected' is a 'constitutive moment' of power in the modern democratic polity as much as it was in all the totalitarian states on record. But the modern democratic state, which happened to be also a capitalist and market society, situated itself almost from the start, or at least from a comparatively early stage, as an agency set to *reduce* fear or *eliminate* it altogether from the life of its subjects/citizens. Uncertainty did not need to be manufactured. State-administered means of violence and repression could be used just on extraordinary occasions, and for most of the time left to rust; there was more than enough inborn, authentic fear emanating from the life conditions of most members of the democratic polity.

The story of the rise of modern democracy could be written in terms of the progress made in eliminating, or constraining and taming, successive causes of uncertainty, anxiety and fear. The long crusade against socially begotten and gestated terrors culminated in collective, state-endorsed insurance against individually suffered misfortune (like unemployment, invalidity, disease or old age), and in collectively guaranteed provision, similarly countersigned by the state, of the amenities essential to individual self-formation and self-assertion, which was the substance, or at least the guiding objective, of the social (misnamed as 'welfare') state. A little more than half a century ago Franklin Delano Roosevelt, in his declaration of the ends of war made in the name of the democratic alliance, announced the coming of a world in which fear itself would be the only remaining calamity of which its inhabitants would still be afraid; in most liberal democracies, the postwar 'glorious thirty years' passed in a concentrated effort to make that promise hold.

With the social state everywhere in retreat, Roosevelt's promise is seldom repeated, and most significantly not by the people at the helm of state power; whereas all the fears which were to have been banished once and for all by the rising social state are back – and with a vengeance; most notably, the fear of social degradation, with the spectre of poverty and social exclusion at the end of the downward slide.

Of the passage from the 'embourgeoisement of the proletariat', viewed with concern and sorrow by the nostalgic left and leftish intellectuals of the postwar years, to the 'proletarianization of the bourgeoisie' in post-Reagan America, Richard Rorty had the following to say:

> Since 1973, the assumption that all hardworking American married couples would be able to afford a home, and that the wife could then, if she chose, stay home and raise kids, has begun to seem absurd. The question now is whether the average married couple, both working full time, will ever be able to take home more than 30,000 dollars a year. If husband and wife each work 2,000 hours a year for the current average wage of production and nonsuper-

visory workers (7.50 dol. per hour), they will make that much. But 30,000 dollars a year will not permit homeownership or buy decent daycare. In a country that believes neither in public transportation nor in national health insurance, this income permits a family of four only a humiliating, hand-to-mouth existence. Such a family, trying to get by on this income, will be constantly tormented by fears of wage rollbacks and downsizing, and of the disastrous consequences of even a brief illness.[36]

And as the *New York Times* reported on 3 March 1996, 72 per cent of Americans believed then that 'layoffs and loss of jobs in this country will continue indefinitely'. They believe that still, and probably more firmly than a dozen years ago; after all, their experience of living on a seesaw is already becoming lifelong. That belief happens to be one of the few popular beliefs that day in, day out find ample corroboration and few if any reasons for self-doubt. And holding such a belief means to be afraid – chronically, day and night, day in, day out.

Sixty years later Roosevelt's declaration of a 'war on fears' (fears of unfreedom, religious persecution, and poverty) and promise of their imminent demise were replaced by George W. Bush's declaration of 'war on terrorism' and promise that it will continue for a long time yet (some of his closest collaborators being still more blunt, warning that it will never end . . .). In the post-Reagan years, it tends to be the fear of threats to personal safety (from terrorists, joined intermittently, though currently somewhat less often than before 9/11, by street beggars, drug-pushers, muggers, and more generally by the conveniently under-defined and so even more horrifying category of the 'underclass', as well as by fast-food poisons, obesity, cholesterol or other people's cigarette smoke) that is designated as a sponge to soak up, absorb and wipe out all other fears. A few years *before* 9/11, Rorty observed (prophetically, as it seems now, *after* 9/11) that 'if the proles can be distracted from their own despair by media-created pseudo-events, including the occasional brief and bloody war, the super-rich will have little to fear.'[37]

But the super-rich have little to fear anyway . . . As Max Hastings rightly points out,

> The haves' most powerful weapon is globalism. Once one passes
> a certain corporate threshold, taxation becomes voluntary, as

Rupert Murdoch's accountants can testify. Confronted with any fiscal or even physical threat, it is easy to move cash or oneself elsewhere. Recognising this, few national governments have the stomach to risk alienating wealth-creators by attacking their bank accounts . . . [Only] a meltdown of the financial system on an unprecedented scale could threaten the security of the rich.[38]

Members of the global elite of super-rich may find themselves now and then *in* this or that place, but nowhere and at no time are they *of* that place – or any other place, to be sure. They need not concern themselves with assuaging the fears that haunt the natives/locals of the place where they stopped for a while, because keeping 'the proles happy' is no longer a condition of their own security (which can be, if need be, sought and found elsewhere), or indeed of their wealth and continuing aggrandisement (which has become eminently light and mobile and can be easily transferred to more benign and hospitable places). If the volume of local fears grows too large for comfort, there are so many other localities to move away to, letting the natives stew and burn alone in the cauldrons of panic and nightmares . . .

For the global elite, whipping up rather than mitigating the fears of locals (any locals, of any locality the elite happens to have chosen for a stopover) spells few if any risks. Refashioning and refocusing the fears born of global social insecurity into local safety concerns seem indeed to be a most effective and almost foolproof strategy; it brings so many gains and relatively few risks, when it is consistently pursued. By far its most important benefit, though, consists in diverting the eyes of the frightened from the causes of their existential anxiety, so that – to quote Hastings again – the global overclass may 'continue rewarding itself on a staggering scale', undisturbed.

Thanks to negative globalization, the sum total, volume and intensity of popular fears amenable to being capitalized on by the promoters and practitioners of that strategy all grow unabated; and thanks to the abundance of fears, the strategy in question can be routinely deployed, and so negative globalization can also continue unabated. For the *foreseeable* future, that is. But then, as we have seen before, 'foreseeability' is one of those attributes which the negatively globalized liquid modern world most conspicuously lacks.

6

Thought against Fear
(or, an inconclusive conclusion
for those who may ask
what might be done)

Sharing with his readers the three shocks he experienced in 1990
when he learned in quick succession of the departures of Althusser,
Benoist and Loreau, Jacques Derrida observed that each death is
the end of *a world*, and each time it is the end of a *unique* world,
a world that can never again reappear or be resurrected.[1] Each
death is *a loss* of a world – a loss *forever*, an *irreparable* loss.
Death is, we may say, the experiential and epistemological foundation of the idea of *uniqueness*.

Ralph Miliband's departure was a particularly cruel and painful
shock to thinking people who rejected the panglossian belief that
everything that could be done to make the planet less threatening
and frightening to humans and so more hospitable to human and
humane life had been already done, and who refused to accept
that no further improvement was conceivable. His own, unique
and inimitable world was a world of undying hope. For that
reason it remains, however, also an indispensable part and a
source of perpetual enrichment of our own worlds. It is the task
of the living to keep hope alive; or rather to resurrect it in a rapidly
changing world prominent for rapidly changing the conditions
under which the ongoing struggle to make it more hospitable to
humanity is conducted.

Ralph Miliband's work stood for the momentous challenge
confronted by the intellectuals of his time (intellectuals: those
thinking people who went on believing that the ultimate purpose

of thought is to make the world better than they found it), and for the ways and means by which the people called 'intellectuals' tried, with mixed success and more than a few blunders, to respond to that challenge.

The challenge in question was the slow yet relentless (though long overlooked and deliberately unacknowledged for longer still) decomposition of the 'historical agent' which the intellectuals hoped (mindful of the 'organic' standards set for them by Antonio Gramsci's code of conduct, and painfully aware of the limited practical effects of pure thought) would usher in (or be ushered into) a land in which the leap towards liberty, equality and fraternity adumbrated in pristine form by thinkers of Enlightenment, but later diverted into capitalist or the communists cul-de-sacs, would finally reach its socialist destination.

In the two centuries or so of their (modern) history, intellectuals travelled all the way from the self-confidence and audacity of young Icarus to the scepticism and circumspection of the elderly Daedalus (a journey, let this be clear, which has not as yet ended, while its path has thus far been and is likely to remain anything but a straight line . . .). And along the whole spectrum of projects, attitudes and *Weltanschauungen* born, dying and abandoned along that path – from the self-confidence, courage and boisterousness of overweening youth (when Claude-Henri Saint-Simon called on his fellow 'positive intellectuals' 'to unify and combine their forces to launch a general and definitive assault against prejudices, and to begin organizing the industrial system') and up to the advanced age of coming-to-one's-senses, caution and judiciousness (when Ludwig Wittgenstein concluded, resignedly, that 'philosophy leaves everything as it was') – they always tacitly suspected or loudly bewailed the impotence of 'pure thought'. Are words able to change the world? Is telling the truth enough to assure its victory over the lie? Is reason capable of standing its own against prejudice and superstition? Is evil likely ever to surrender to the shining glory of goodness, or ugliness to the blinding splendours of beauty?

Intellectuals never really trusted in their own powers to make the word flesh. They needed someone to perform the job they urged should be undertaken. Someone with real power to do things and ensure that they continue on once they are done (does not knowledge need power to make a difference to the world, as much as power needs knowledge to change the world in the right way and to the right purpose?). The 'enlightened despot', the wise yet ruthless, and above all resourceful Prince able to recast the advice of Reason into binding Law, was the obvious first choice of the intellectuals. But the first among many to follow; history saw to it that once chosen he ceased to be an obvious, let alone promising choice. Relations between the powers-that-be and their zealous counsellors (all too often viewed as overzealous by those to whom the advice was addressed) were ambivalent at best, and most of the time stormy and poisoned by mutual suspicion. The marriage of the self-appointed law *designers* with the power-holding law *makers* soon proved to be of the hate–love sort, incurably frail and always on the verge of divorce.

For at least a century, the prime intellectual choice for the role of the 'historical agent' of emancipation was a collective hoped to be (or believed to have already been) put together and cemented out of a rather variegated assortment of skills and trades, summarily categorized as the 'working class'. Forced to sell their labouring/creative capacity at a fraudulent price and falling victim to the denial of human dignity which went together with such a sale, the working class was expected to rise or be lifted from a merely 'objective', unthinking existence of a 'class in itself' to the rank of a 'class for itself': become aware of its historical destination, embrace it, turn itself (or be turned) from an object into a subject (*the* subject of history, as it were) and unite in a revolution aimed to put an end to their suffering. Since, however, the causes of their misery had systemic roots, that class of sufferers, according to Karl Marx's unforgettable sentence, was a unique class of people who could not emancipate themselves without emancipating the whole of human society; nor could it end its specific class-bound misery without putting an end to all and any human misery. Once ascribed such potency, the working class offered a natural and secure haven for hope; so much more secure than the imaginary faraway cities where the writers of early modern utopias placed the 'enlightened despots', expected and trusted to legislate happiness on their unwitting and originally also unwilling subjects.

Whether the ascription was or was not warranted was a moot question from the start. It could be argued that – contrary to

Marx's belief – the restlessness on the factory floors of early capitalism was prompted more by a loss of security than by a love of freedom, and that once the lost and bewailed security was regained or rebuilt on a new and different foundation, it was inevitable that the unrest would boil away, stopping well short of its allegedly revolutionary/emancipatory destination. It could be argued as well that the recycling of dispossessed craftsmen, farm tenants and many other hands forced to be idle into an apparently homogeneous working class was a step that was more power-assisted than self-made, and that economic powers could decompose that class in just the same way as they were once instrumental in putting it together . . .

These and numerous other caveats were easier to make with the benefit of hindsight, however – *after* the evidence had accumulated that far from being a preliminary step towards the revolutionary overhaul of the power system, such manifestations of 'class struggle' as collective bargaining practices and the deployment of 'nuisance capacity' in defence of wage differentials were aimed at targets placed well *inside* the limits of capital–labour relations, and would not break out of the confines of the capitalist order – let alone break the order itself. And *after*, in addition, the possibility became gradually yet steadily ever more credible that by contributing to a regular, nearly routine correction of intolerable and hence potentially explosive systemic deformities, labour struggles served as a homeostatic, stabilizing, 'equilibrium restoring' device, rather than disrupting, let alone undermining, the capitalist order.

After a long period of initial unrest associated with the melting of premodern economic structures came the period of 'relative stability' – underpinned by the emergent, but apparently solid structures of industrial society. The politically administered instruments of the 'recommodification of capital and labour' became a constant feature of the capitalist world – with states playing an active role in 'pump priming', promoting and ensuring the intensive and extensive expansion of the capitalist economy on the one side, and in reconditioning and rehabilitating labour on the other. However harsh the hardships suffered at the receiving end of capitalist expansion, and however disconcerting the perpetual fears of periodic bouts of economic depression, frameworks able to accommodate lifelong expectations and projects, and equipped with tested and trustworthy repair tools, appeared firmly set – allowing for the long-term planning of individual lives, grounded in a rising feeling of security and confidence in the future. Capital and labour, locked in apparently unbreakable mutual dependency, increasingly convinced of the permanence of their mutual bond and certain to 'meet again and again' in the times to come, sought and found a mutually beneficial and promising, or at least tolerable, settlement; a mode of cohabitation punctuated by repetitive tugs-of-war, but also by rounds of successful, since for a time mutually satisfactory, renegotiation of the rules of cooperation.

Frustrated by and impatient with the way things seemed to be going, Lenin complained that if they were left to their own devices workers would only develop a 'trade union mentality' and remain far too narrow-minded, egocentric and divided to face up to their historic mission, let alone perform it. The same trend which exasperated Lenin, inventor and ardent advocate of 'short cuts' and of the substitution of the meticulously prepared takeover of power by 'professional revolutionaries' for unreliable spontaneous explosions of proletarian anger, was also spotted, but viewed with mildly optimistic equanimity, by his contemporary Eduard Bernstein – the founder (with considerable help from the Fabians) of the 'revisionist' programme of accommodation and the pursuit of socialist values and ambitions inside the political and economic framework of an essentially capitalist society: of gradual but steady 'amelioration' rather than a revolutionary, one-off overhaul of the status quo.

Lenin's and Bernstein's diagnoses were strikingly similar – but their responses to the question of 'if so, what is there to be done?' were radically different. True, both remained faithful to Marx's proposition that marriage with practice is the sole therapy for the endemic weaknesses of thought, and to his choice of the partner to be united with the emancipatory theory at the imminent wedding ('let those who think meet those who suffer'). But while Bernstein visualized the intellectuals' role on the pattern of a loyal and obedient housewife, Lenin allocated the roles differently: it was theory that should play first fiddle and rule inside the married couple, arming itself for that purpose through the appropriation of much, most, or all of the sturdiness, muscle and tenacity normally imputed to its macho husband. To achieve that purpose, however, those who knew what is to be done needed to transform themselves from a debating society into a tightly integrated, mercilessly disciplined and ruthless body of 'professional revolutionaries', aware that (in Alain Finkielkraut's poignant description of that creed) 'concepts are in the street, arguments in the events, and reason in the drama in which men are actors before they became thinkers'.[2] It is the proletariat who will ultimately remake reality according to the rules of reason and the principles of justice – but it won't do that unless it is goaded, pushed and otherwise coerced by those who know and/or codify those rules and principles. Workers need to be forced to perform the ultimate act of liberation which – by a verdict of history with no appeal allowed – has been their mission from the start of the class war, but which they would be too indolent or slothful, or too naive and too easily duped, to perform – unless called to arms and coerced to act . . .

Lenin's bold/desperate move shifted the intellectuals, as 'knowers of history', from the design office to the controlling desk of the revolution. They were to transform *themselves* into historical actors by putting the actor-collective appointed by history under their direct command and then beating, kneading and drilling that collective into a tightly disciplined army of war and/or a weapon of mass destruction.

Lenin's move was perhaps intended as a bid to liberate the intellectuals from their original affliction of impotence: to prompt them to reconstitute themselves into the collective 'historical actor' which the intellectuals, haunted by fears of their own impotence, had been thus far seeking outside their ranks. This time the actor was not to be imagined or postulated, but all too real, and not the prospective object of intellectual enlightenment and guidance, but a ruthless boss, omniscient from the start and ever more omnipotent, demanding obedience, self-renunciation and unconditional surrender. Whatever its intentions, Lenin's stratagem proved in practice to be only a change of management in that scheme of things that lay behind the intellectuals' trauma of inborn weakness. The Party – produced by the intellectuals reconstituting themselves as the 'historical actor' – took over from the 'suffering and humiliated masses' as the reference point for intellectual services; unlike the proletarian masses it replaced in the role of mover of history, the Party did not want (nor was it to allow even a mere supposition of wanting) any enlightenment and guidance from outside. It demanded instead self-effacement, sub-servience, obsequiousness and servility. It needed martinets, not teachers. Servants, not guides.

Were the hard times which befell the former legislators, the descendants of the *philosophes* and executors of their bequest, of their own making? Did they ask for trouble all along from the moment their search for the historical actor had started? They dreamt of a world of complete transparency and total order. They did not know that 'complete transparency' comes together with complete surveillance and that 'total order' belongs to the dreams and purposes of totalitarianism, commandants of concentration camps and cemetery management. They got what they helped to bring into being – and what they did not bargain for.

Marx insisted that the capital enslaving labour was nothing but alienated labour power. Was the party anything other than the alienation of the intellectuals' thinking powers?

As had happened with the way leading from the word to flesh, so the tract leading from the despair of impotence to the joys of self-importance was now to be transferred, and for a long time to come mediated by the Party and under its exclusive management.

As developments kept confirming Lenin's sombre and Bern-stein's sanguine anticipations, György Lukács explained the evident reluctance of history to follow Marx's original prognosis with a concept coined for the purpose (though harking back to Plato's allegory of the shadows cast on the walls of the cave), the concept of 'false consciousness', insidiously inspired, by the 'fraud-ulent totality' of the capitalist social order, which promotes and won't fail to promote it – unless counteracted by the efforts of the Party, which can see through the deceitful appearances into the inexorable truth of historical laws and then, after the pattern of Plato's philosophers, share its discoveries with the deluded cave-dwellers.

When it is combined with Antonio Gramsci's concepts of the Party as the 'collective intellectual' as well as of 'organic intellec-tuals' articulating class interests in order to serve the class whose interests they articulated, Lukács's reinterpretation of the vagaries of post-Marx history ostensibly elevated the historical role of intellectuals, and so also their ethical/political responsibility, to new heights. But by the same token, a Pandora's box of reciprocal accusations, imputations of guilt and suspicions of treachery was thrown open, ushering in a long era of charges of *trahisons des clercs*, uncivil wars, mutual defamation, witch-hunting and character assassination. Indeed, if the labour movement sometime, somewhere failed to behave in line with its prognosticated historical mission, and particularly if it shied away from the revolutionary overturn of the capitalist power, the only ones to blame were the would-be but failed 'organic intellectuals' who had neglected or even actively betrayed their duty to condense (and subsequently dissolve) themselves into the right kind of a party.

Paradoxically, the publicly acknowledged, self-appointed, aspiring or failed intellectuals found the temptation to adopt such an unflattering view of themselves difficult to resist, since it converted even their most spectacular displays of theoretical weakness and practical impotence into powerful arguments which obliquely though perversely reasserted their key historical role. I remember, shortly after coming to Britain, listening to a Ph.D. student who, after perusing a few of Sidney and Beatrice Webb's writings, hurried to proclaim, to the unqualified approval of the tightly packed seminar audience, that the reasons why the socialist revolution had tarryied so abominably in arriving in Britain were all there, in those books.

There was writing on the wall which, if only it had been spotted in time, and read carefully and with an unprejudiced eye, would have cast doubt on this intellectualist conceit. The thoughts of Lukács or Gramsci, freshly discovered by the British intellectual left, did not however help to decode the messages the writing conveyed. How to link, say, student unrest to the winter of discontent? What in fact was one witnessing – battles at the rear waged by troops in retreat and close to capitulation, or forward units of advancing, ever more boisterous armies? Were they distant echoes of old battles and belated restagings of aged scenarios, or prodromal signs and augury of new wars to come? Symptoms of an end, or a beginning? And if a beginning, then the beginning of what?

The news of the latest intellectual stirrings abroad only added to the bewilderment and confusion, as announcements of a 'farewell to proletariat' drifted from beyond the Channel together with

Althusser's reminders that the time had finally matured for revolutionary action. E. P. Thomson's enchantingly romantic vision of the working class's immaculate self-conception was met with a frontal assault by the editors of the *New Left Review* for its theoretical poverty (meaning, probably, the conspicuous absence of intellectuals in Thompson's edifying tale).

It would be dishonest and misleading to claim retrospectively one's own advance wisdom. It would also be dishonest, unjust and not at all illuminating to blame those locked into the fast-running affairs for their confusion. However the blame and exonerations are allocated, the fact remains that the impending end of the 'glorious thirty years' (as the three postwar decades of the construction of the social state have been retrospectively described, though only after the conditions that made them feasible had dissipated or been taken apart, and only when it had become blatantly obvious that they had) threw the familiar world out of joint and made the tested tools which had been used to scrutinize and describe that world useless. The time of hunches and guesses had arrived, and of a lot of confusion. Orthodoxies were dug into ever deeper trenches and surrounded by barbed wire, while heresies, growing thicker on the ground, gained in courage and impertinence even while seeking in vain for a common language and moving nowhere near to consensus.

The source of this intellectual disarray, explicitly pointed to by some and glossed over by others, was, let me repeat, the apparent disappearance of the heretofore indisputable historical agent (as the hub round which all strategies, however at odds with each other, ultimately rotated) – perceived at first on the intellectual left as a growing separation from and breakdown of communication with 'the movement'. As the theoretically impeccable postulates and prognoses were one by one refuted by events, intellectual circles (with only a few exceptions – some resisting the trend consistently, others sporadically, when there was 'secondary picketing' or when ad hoc groups were formed in spiritual support of the miners vainly trying to escape the Thatcherist juggernaut) turned ever more zealously and conspicuously to self-referential interests and pursuits, as if in obedience to Michel Foucault's proclamation of the advent of 'specific intellectuals' (and so also 'specific', that is professionally divided and split, politics).

Whether the concept of specific or specialized intellectuals could be anything other than an oxymoron was of course then, as it is now, a moot question. But whether or not the application of the term 'intellectual' is legitimate in the case of university lecturers visiting the public arena solely on the occasions of successive disagreements on university salaries, or artists protesting about successive cuts in subsidies for theatrical productions or film-making, or consultants going on strike against excessive demands on their services, one thing is certain: to these new, institutionally circumscribed, self-centred and self-referential varieties of political stand-taking and power struggles the figure of the 'historical agent' is completely irrelevant. It can be dropped from the agenda without a guilty conscience, and above all without regrets and the bitter aftertaste of loss.

Must the hopes and the job of emancipation follow the vanishing 'historical agent' into the abyss, as the sinking Captain Ahab beckoned his sailors to do? I would argue that the work of Theodore W. Adorno can be reread as one long and thorough attempt to confront that question and to justify an emphatic 'no' as the answer.

After all, long before the passions of British intellectuals for a historical agent started to dull and wilt, Adorno warned his older friend Walter Benjamin against what he called 'Brechtian motifs': the hope that the 'actual workers' would save arts from the loss of their aura or be saved by the 'immediacy of the combined aesthetic effect' of revolutionary art.[3] The 'actual workers', he insisted, 'in fact enjoy no advantage over their bourgeois counterpart' in this respect – they 'bear all the marks of mutilation of the typical bourgeois character'. And then came the parting shot: beware of 'making our necessity' (that is the necessity of the intellectuals who 'need the proletarian for the revolution') 'into a virtue of the proletariat as we are constantly tempted to do'.

At the same time, Adorno insisted that though the prospects of human emancipation, focused on the idea of a different and better society, now appear less encouraging than those which seemed so evident to Marx, the charges raised by Marx against a world unforgivably inimical to humanity have not lost any of their topicality, and no competent jury has found any proof of the unreality of the original emancipating ambitions that it would recognize as clinching. There is therefore no sufficient, let alone necessary, reason, Adorno insisted, to take emancipation off the agenda. If anything, the contrary is the case: the noxious persistence of social ills is one more and admittedly powerful reason to try still harder.

I suggest that Adorno's admonition is as topical today as it was when it was first written down: 'The undiminished presence of suffering, fear and menace necessitates that the thought that cannot be realized should not be discarded.' Now as then, 'philosophy must come to know, without any mitigation, why the world – which could be paradise here and now – can become hell itself tomorrow'. The difference between 'now' and 'then' has to be sought elsewhere than in the notion that the task of emancipation has lost its urgency or that the dream of emancipation has been found idle.

What Adorno hastened however to add was the following: if to Marx the world seemed prepared to turn into a paradise 'there and then' and appeared to be ready for an instantaneous U-turn, and if it looked therefore as if 'the possibility of changing the world "from top to bottom" was immediately present',[4] this is no longer the case, if it ever was ('only stubbornness can still maintain the thesis as Marx formulated it'). It is the possibility of a *short cut* to a world better fit for human habitation that has been lost from view and seems to be more unreal than before.

One could also say that there are no passable bridges left between this world here and now and that other, 'emancipated' world, hospitable to humanity and 'user friendly'. There are no crowds eager to stampede the whole length of the bridge were such a bridge to be designed, or vehicles waiting to take the willing to the other side and deliver them safely to their destination. No one can be sure how a usable bridge could be designed and where along the shore the bridgehead could be located to facilitate smooth and suitable traffic. The possibilities, one has to conclude, are *not* immediately present.

'The world wants to be deceived' – Adorno's blunt verdict sounds like a commentary to Lion Feuchtwanger's doleful story of Odysseus and the swine who refused to return to their previous human shape because they detested the worry of making decisions and taking responsibility which the condition of being human necessarily involved, or for that matter Erich Fromm's 'escape from freedom', or else the archetype of them all, Plato's melancholy speculation on the tragic fate of philosophers trying to share with the cavemen the good tidings brought from the sunlit world of pure ideas. 'People are not only, as the saying goes, falling for the swindle ... [T]hey desire a deception ... [T]hey sense that their lives would be completely intolerable as soon as they no longer clung to satisfactions which are none at all.'[5]

Adorno quotes with unreserved approval Sigmund Freud's essay on group psychology. The group, he writes, 'wishes to be governed by unrestricted force: it has extreme passion for authority: in Le Bon's phrase, it has a thirst for obedience. The primal father is the group ideal, which governs the ego in the place of the ego ideal.'[6]

In Adorno's words, 'spirit' and 'concrete entity' have parted ways and the spirit can cling to realities only at its own peril, and so ultimately at the peril of reality itself.

> Only a thinking that has no mental sanctuary, no illusion of an inner realm, and that acknowledged its lack of function and power can perhaps catch a glimpse of an order of the possible and the nonexistent, where human beings and things would be in their rightful place.[7]

> Philosophical thinking begins as soon as it ceases to content itself with cognitions that are predictable and from which nothing more emerges than what had been placed there beforehand.[8]

> Thinking is not the intellectual reproduction of what already exists anyway. As long as it doesn't break off, thinking has a secure hold on possibility. Its insatiable aspect, its aversion to being quickly and easily satisfied, refuses the foolish wisdom of resignation. The utopian moment in thinking is stronger the less it ... objectifies itself into a utopia and hence sabotages its realization. Open thinking points beyond itself.[9]

Philosophy, Adorno insists, means the 'determination to hang on to intellectual and real freedom', and only on that condition may it, as it should, remain 'immune to the suggestion of the status quo'.[10]

'Theory', Adorno concludes, 'speaks for what is not narrow-minded.'[11] Practice, and *practicality* in particular, is more often than not an excuse or a self-deception of 'scoundrels', like that 'idiotic parliamentarian in Doré's caricature', who is proud of not looking beyond the immediate tasks. Adorno denies practice the esteem that tends to be lavishly poured upon it by the spokesmen

for 'positive' science and those professionals of academic philosophy (indeed, an overwhelming majority of them) who surrender
to their terror.

If 'emancipation', the supreme objective of social critique, aims
at 'the development of autonomous, independent individuals who
judge and decide consciously for themselves,'[12] it is up against the
awesome resistance of 'culture industry'; but also against the pressure of that multitude whose cravings that industry promises to
gratify (and, genuinely or deceitfully, does).

So where does all that leave the prospects, the tasks, the strategies
of the intellectuals, as long as they are and wish to remain the
guardians of the unfulfilled hopes and promises of the past, and
critics of a present guilty of forgetting them and abandoning them
unfulfilled?

By common opinion, inaugurated it seems by Jürgen Habermas
and contested by only a few of the Adorno scholars and only relatively recently, Adorno's answer to these and similar questions is
best conveyed by the image of a 'message in a bottle'. Whoever
wrote the message and put it in, sealed the bottle and threw it
into the sea had no idea when (if ever) and which (if any) sailor
would spot the bottle and fish it out; and whether that sailor,
uncorking the bottle and pulling out the piece of paper it con-
tained, would be able and willing to read the text, understand the
message, accept its content and put it to the kind of use the author
intended. The entire equation consists of unknown variables, and
there is no way the author of the 'message in a bottle' can resolve
it. He can, at best, repeat after Marx: *Dixi et salvavi animam
meam* – the author has fulfilled his mission and done all in her
or his power to save the message from extinction. The hopes and
promises the author knew, but most of her or his contemporaries
never learned or preferred to forget, will not pass a point of no
return on their way to oblivion; they will be given at least a chance
of another lease of life. They will not die intestate together with
the author – at least will not *have* to die, as die they *must* were
the thinker to surrender to the mercy of the waves instead of
reaching for a hermetically sealed bottle.

As Adorno warns, and repeatedly, 'no thought is immune
against communication, and to utter it in the wrong place and in
wrong agreement is enough to undermine its truth.'[13] And so,

when it comes to communicating with the actors, with the would-be actors, with abortive actors and those people who are reluctant to join the action in their own time, 'for the intellectual, inviolable isolation is now the only way of showing some measure of solidarity' for those 'down and out'.

Such self-inflicted seclusion is not in Adorno's view an act of treachery – neither a sign of withdrawal, nor a gesture of condescension, nor both ('condescension, and thinking oneself no better, are the same', as he himself points out). Keeping a distance, paradoxically, is an act of engagement – in the only form which engagement on the side of unfulfilled or betrayed hopes may sensibly take: 'The detached observer is as much entangled as the active participant; the only advantage of the former is insight into his entanglement, and the infinitesimal freedom that lies in knowledge as such.'[14]

The 'message in a bottle' allegory implies two presumptions: that there was a message fit to be written down and worthy of the trouble needed to set the bottle afloat; and that at the time it is found and read (at a time which cannot be defined in advance) the message will still be worthy of the founder's effort to unpack it and study, absorb and adopt it. In some cases, like Adorno's, entrusting the message to the unknown reader of an undefined future may be preferred to consorting with contemporaries who are deemed unready or unwilling to listen to, let alone grasp and retain, what they hear. In such cases, sending the message into unmapped space and unknown time rests on the hope that its potency will outlive its current neglect and survive the (transient) conditions that caused the negligence. The *'message in a bottle' expedient makes sense if (and only if) someone who resorts to it trusts values to be eternal, believes truths to be universal, and suspects that the worries that currently trigger the search for truth and the rallying in defence of values will persist.* The message in a bottle is a testimony to the *transience of frustration* and the *duration of hope*, to the *indestructibility of possibilities* and the *frailty of the adversities* that barred them from implementation. In Adorno's rendition, critical theory is such a testimony – and this warrants the metaphor of the message in a bottle.

In the 'Postscript' to his last magnum opus, *La Misère du Monde*,[15] Bourdieu pointed out that the numbers of personalities on the political stage who can comprehend and articulate the expectations and demands of their electors is shrinking fast; the political space is inward focused and bent on closing in on itself. It needs to be thrown open again, and this can only be done through bringing 'private' troubles and cravings, often inchoate and inarticulate, into direct relevance to the political process (and, consequently, vice versa).

This is easier said than done, though, because public discourse is inundated with Émile Durkheim's 'prénotions' – presumptions rarely spelled out overtly and even less frequently scrutinized, uncritically deployed whenever subjective experience is raised to the level of public discourse and whenever private troubles are categorized, recycled in public discourse and re-represented as public issues. To do its service to human experience, *sociology needs to begin with clearing the site*. Critical assessment of tacit or vociferous *prénotions* must proceed together with an effort to make visible and audible the aspects of experience that normally stay beyond individual horizons, or below the threshold of individual awareness.

A moment of reflection will show, though, that to bring an awareness of the mechanisms that render life painful or even unliveable does not mean they are already neutralized; to draw the contradictions into the light does not mean they are resolved. A long and tortuous road stretches between recognition of the roots of trouble and their eradication, and taking the first step in no way ensures that further steps will be taken, let alone that the road will be followed to the end. And yet there is no denying the crucial importance of the beginning – of laying bare the complex network of causal links between pains suffered individually and conditions collectively produced. In sociology, and still more in a sociology which strives to be up to its task, the beginning is even more decisive than elsewhere; it is this first step that designates and paves the road to rectification which otherwise would not exist, let alone be noticed.

Indeed, we need to repeat after Pierre Bourdieu: '*those who have the chance of dedicating their lives to the study of the social world cannot rest, neutral and indifferent, in front of the struggles of which the future of the world is the stake*'.[16]

Their (our, the sociologists') duty, in other words, is the duty to hope. But what are we to hope for?

As has been stated before, neither of the twin accusations raised by Karl Marx against capital almost two centuries ago – its wastefulness and its moral iniquity – has lost any of its topicality. Only the scope of waste and injustice has changed: both have acquired by now *planetary dimensions*. And so has the formidable task of emancipation – its urgency prompted the establishment of the Frankfurt Institute more than half a century ago, guiding its labours since, and also animated Ralph Miliband's life and work.

Let me note however that it is the increasingly 'transnational' knowledge elite, the ever more assertively and blatantly *extraterritorial* class of symbol-makers and symbol manipulators, that stand in the forefront of 'globalization' – that shorthand for the genuine or putative, gradual yet relentless weakening of most territorially fixed distinctions and the replacement of territorially defined groups and associations with electronically mediated 'networks', careless of physical space and cut loose from the hold of localities and locally circumscribed sovereignties. And let me note that it is the knowledge elite, first and foremost, that experiences its own condition as 'transnational', and that it is such experience which it tends to reprocess into the idea of 'global culture' and of 'hybridization' (the updated denomination for the discredited notion of the 'melting pot') as its dominant trend; an image that the less mobile remainder of humanity might well find difficult to adopt as a fair representation of their own daily realities.

The compact between 'the intellectuals' and the 'people' whom they once undertook to uplift and guide into history, freedom and the courage of self-assertion, has been broken – or rather revoked as unilaterally as it was announced at the threshold of the modern era. The descendants of the intellectuals of yore, the present-day 'knowledge elite', having shared in the 'secession of the contented', now move in a world sharply different from, and certainly not overlapping with, the many and different worlds in which the lives and the prospects (or their absence) of the 'people' are ensconced and locked.

Adorno's precept that the task of critical thought 'is not the conservation of the past, but the redemption of the hopes of the past' has lost nothing of its topicality; but it is precisely because it is topical under circumstances which have radically changed that critical thought needs continuous rethinking in order to remain up to its task. Two themes must be assigned pride of place on the agenda of rethinking.

First, the hope and chance of striking an acceptable balance between freedom and security, those two not self-evidently compatible yet equally crucial, *sine qua non* conditions of humane society, need to be placed at the centre of the rethinking effort. And second, among the hopes of the past that need to be most urgently redeemed, those preserved in Kant's own 'message in a bottle', his *Ideen zur eine allgemeine Geschichte in weltbürgerliche Absicht*, can rightly claim meta-hope status: of a hope that can make – will make, ought to make – the bold act of hoping possible. Whatever new balance between freedom and security is sought, it needs to be envisaged on a planetary scale.

I write 'must' (a verb that ought be used only in extreme circumstances) because the alternative to paying heed, and urgently, to Kant's prophetic warnings is what Jean-Pierre Dupuy described as 'unavoidable catastrophe', while pointing out that prophesying the advent of that catastrophe as passionately and vociferously as we can manage is the sole chance of making the unavoidable avoidable – and perhaps even the inevitable impossible to happen.[17] 'We are condemned to perpetual vigilance', he warns. A lapse of vigilance may prove a sufficient (though only a necessary, *sine qua non*) condition of the catastrophe's inevitability; proclaiming that inevitability and so 'thinking of the continuation' of the human presence on Earth 'as of the negation of autodestruction' is, on the other hand, a necessary (and hopefully the sufficient) condition of the 'unavoidable future not happening'.

Prophets drew their sense of mission, their determination to follow that mission as well as their ability to see it through, from believing in what Dupuy wishes us to believe in faced by the catastrophe presently threatening. After all, they hammered home the imminence of the apocalypse not because they dreamed of academic laurels and therefore wished their power of prediction to be vindicated, but because they *wished the future to prove them wrong*, and because they saw no other way to prevent the catastrophe from happening except letting – forcing – their prophecies to refute themselves.

We may prophesy that, unless bridled and tamed, our negative globalization, alternating between stripping the free of their security and offering security in the form of unfreedom, makes catastrophe *inescapable*. Without this prophecy being made and without treating it seriously, humanity can harbour little hope of rendering it *avoidable*. The only promising start to a therapy against rising and ultimately incapacitating fear is to see through it, down to its roots – because the only promising way to continue with it requires facing up to the task of cutting out those roots.

The coming century may well be a time of ultimate catastrophe. Or it may be a time when a new compact between intellectuals and the people – now meaning humanity at large – is negotiated and brought to life. Let's hope that the choice between these two futures is still ours.

Notes

Introduction

1 Lucien Febvre, *Le Problème de l'incroyance au XVIe siècle*, A. Michel, 1942, p. 380.
2 Quoted after Alain Finkielkraut, *Nous autres, modernes*, Ellipses, 2005, p. 249.
3 Hugues Lagrange, *La Civilité à l'épreuve. Crime et sentiment d'insécurité*, PUF, 1996, pp. 173ff.
4 See Craig Brown, *1966 and All That*, Hodder and Stoughton, 2005; here quoted after the edited extract in *Guardian Weekend*, 5 Nov. 2005, p. 73.
5 See Thomas Mathiesen, *Silently Silenced: Essays on the Creation of Acquiescence in Modern Society*, Waterside Press, 2004, pp. 9, 14.
6 Catherine Bennett, 'The time lord', *Guardian Wellbeing Handbook*, 5 Nov. 2005.
7 Milan Kundera, *Les Testaments trahis*, Gallimard, 1990. In English as *Testaments Betrayed*, Faber, 1995.
8 See Jacques Attali, 'Le *Titanic*, le mondial and nous', *Le Monde*, 3 July 1998.
9 See Peter Applebome and Jonathan D. Glater, 'Storm leaves legal system in shambles', *New York Times*, 9 Sept. 2005.
10 See Dan Barry, 'Macabre reminder: the corpse on Union Street', *New York Times*, 8 Sept. 2005.
11 Mary William Walsh, 'Hurricane victims face tighter limits on bankruptcy', *New York Times*, 27 Sept. 2005.

12 See Gary Rivlin, 'New Orleans utility struggles to relight a city of darkness', *New York Times*, 19 Nov. 2005.

13 'Louisiana sees faded urgency in relief effort', *New York Times*, 22 Nov. 2005.

14 Jean-Pierre Dupuy, *Pour un catastrophisme éclairé. Quand l'impossible est certain*, Seuil, 2002, p. 10.

15 Ibid., p. 143.

16 Corinne Lepage and François Guery, *La Politique de précaution*, PUF, 2001, p. 16.

17 Barry, 'Macabre reminder'.

18 Timothy Garton Ash, 'It always lies below', *Guardian*, 8 Sep. 2005.

19 See Stephen Graham, 'Switching cities off: urban infrastructure and US air power', *City*, 2 (2005), pp. 169–94.

20 Martin Pawley, *Terminal Architecture*, Reaktion 1997, p. 162.

21 John Dunn, *Setting the People Free: The Story of Democracy*, Atlantic Books, 2005, p. 161.

22 See Danny Hakim, 'For a G.M. family, the American dream vanishes', *New York Times*, 19 Nov. 2005.

23 Cf Georg Christoph Lichtenberg, *Aphorisms*, trans. R. J. Hollingdale, Penguin, 1990, p. 161.

Chapter 1 Dread of Death

1 See Maurice Blanchot, *The Gaze of Orpheu*, Station Hill, 1981.

2 See Sandra M. Gilbert, *Death's Door: Modern Dying and the Ways we Grieve*, W. W. Norton, 2005.

3 See George L. Mosse, *Fallen Soldiers*, Oxford University Press, 1990, pp. 34ff.

4 Sigmund Freud, 'Thoughts for the time of war and death', in Freud, *Civilization, Society and Religion*, ed. Albert Dickson, Penguin, 1991, pp. 77–8.

5 See Jacques Derrida, *Chaque fois unique, la fin du monde*, presented by Pascale-Anne Brault and Michael Naas, Galilée, 2003.

6 See Vladimir Jankélévitch, *Penser la mort?* Liana Levi, 1994, pp. 10ff.

7 Freud, 'Thoughts for the time of war and death', p. 78.

8 See Jean Baudrillard, *Selected Writings*, ed. Mark Poster, Polity, 1988, p. 168.

9 See my *Liquid Life*, Polity, 2005, ch. 5: 'Consumers in consumer society'.

10 See Jean Starobinski, 'Le concept de nostalgie', in Revue Diogène, *Une Antologie de la vie intellectuelle au XXe siècle*, PUF, 2005, pp. 170ff.

11 See his interview in *Tikkun*, July–Aug. 2005, pp. 39–41.
12 Sigmund Freud, *Civilization and Its Discontents*, collected in Freud, *Civilization, Society, Religion*, p. 264.

Chapter 2   Fear and Evil

1 Susan Neiman, *Evil in Modern Thought: An Alternative History of Philosophy*, Princeton University Press, 2002.
2 Jean-Pierre Dupuy, *Petite métaphysique des tsunamis*, Seuil, 2005.
3 Jean-Jacques Rousseau, 'Lettre à Monsieur de Voltaire', in *Oeuvres complètes*, Pléiade, 1959, vol. 4, p. 1062.
4 Neiman, *Evil in Modern Thought*, p. 230.
5 Ibid., pp. 240, 281.
6 Hannah Arendt, *Eichmann in Jerusalem*, Viking, 1963, p. 277.
7 John P. Sabini and Mary Silver, 'Destroying the innocent with a clear conscience: a sociopsychology of the Holocaust', in *Survivors, Victims, and Perpetrators: Essays in the Nazi Holocaust*, ed. Joel P. Dinsdale, Hemisphere, 1980, p. 330.
8 Neiman, *Evil in Modern Thought*, p. 287.
9 Arendt, *Eichmann in Jerusalem*, p. 295.
10 Hans Mommsen, 'Anti-Jewish politics and the interpretation of the Holocaust', in *The Challenge of the Third Reich: The Adam von Trott Memorial Lectures*, ed. Hedley Bull, Clarendon Press, 1986, p. 117.
11 Arendt, *Eichmann in Jerusalem*, pp. 25–6.
12 See the incisive analysis of Primo Levi's views on that point in Tzvetan Todorov, *Mémoire du mal, tentation du bien*, Robert Laffont, 2000, pp. 260ff.
13 Eduardo Mendietta, 'The axle of evil: SUVing through the slums of globalizing neoliberalism', *City*, 2 (2005), pp. 195–204.

Chapter 3   Horror of the Unmanageable

1 See Jean-Pierre Dupuy, *Pour un catastrophisme éclairé*, Seuil, 2002, and *petite métaphysique des tsunamis*, Seuil, 2005.
2 See Ivan Illich, *Limits to Medicine: Medical Nemesis: The Expropriation of Health*, Oenghin, 1977.
3 Jean Pierre Dupuy, *Petite métaphysique des tsunamis*, Seuil, 2005, p. 43.
4 Paul Taponnier, 'Tsunami: je savait tout, je ne savait rien', *Le Monde*, 5 Jan. 2005.

5   This and the following quotations come from David Gonzales, 'From margins of society to center of the tragedy', *New York Times*, 2 Sept. 2005.

6   See my *Wasted Lives*, Polity, 2004.

7   Simon Shama, 'Sorry Mr President, Katrina is not 9/11', *Guardian* 12 Sept. 2005.

8   See Max Hastings, 'They've never had it so good', *Guardian*, 6 Aug. 2005.

9   See Susan Neiman, *Evil in Modern Thought: An Alternative History of Philosophy*, Princeton University Press, 2002, Introduction.

10 See Max Weber, *Political Writings*, ed. Peter Lasman and Ronald Speirs, Cambridge University Press, 1994, p. 359.

11 Dupuy, *Pour un catastrophisme éclairé*, pp. 76–7.

12 Jodi Dean, 'Communicative capitalism: circulation and the foreclosure of politics', *Cultural Politics*, 1 (2005), pp. 51–73.

13 See Hermann Knell, *To Destroy a City: Strategic Bombing and its Human Consequences in World War II*, Da Capo Press, 2003.

14 Ibid., pp. 25, 330–1.

Chapter 4   Terrors of the Global

1   Arundhati Roy, 'L'Empire n'est pas invulnérable', *Manière de Voir*, no. 75 (June–July 2004), pp. 63–6.

2   Milan Kundera, *L'Art du roman*, Gallimard, 1986.

3   See Jean-Pierre Dupuy, *Pour un catastrophisme éclairé. Quand l'impossible est certain*, Seuil, 2002, p. 154.

4   Robert Castel, *L'Insécurité sociale. Qu'est-ce qu'être protégé?* Seuil, 2003, p. 5.

5   Mark Danner, 'Taking stock of the forever war', *New York Times*, 11 Sept. 2005.

6   Quoted after Matthew J. Morgan, 'The garrison state revisited: civil–military implications of terrorism and security', *Contemporary Politics*, 10, no. 1 (Mar. 2004), pp. 5–19.

7   Michael Meacher, 'Playing Bin Laden's game', *Guardian*, 11 May 2004, p. 21; Adam Curtis quoted from Andy Beckett, 'The making of the terror myth', *Guardian*, 15 Oct. 2004, 42 pp. 2–3.

8   See Richard A. Oppel Jr, Eric Schmitt and Thom Shanker, 'Baghdad bombings raise anew questions about US strategy in Iraq', *New York Times*, 17 Sept. 2005.

9   See 'Generals offer sober outlook on Iraqi war', *New York Times*, 19 May 2005.

10 Gary Young, 'Blair's blowback', *Guardian*, 11 July 2005.

11 See Carlotta Gall, 'Mood of anxiety engulfs Afghans as violence rises', *New York Times*, 30 June 2005.

12 See John F. Burns, 'Iraqi offensive met by wave of new violence from insurgents', *New York Times*, 30 May 2005.

13 See Richard W. Stevenson, 'Acknowledging difficulties, insisting on a fight to the finish', *New York Times*, 29 June 2005.

14 See Dexter Filkins and David S. Cloud, 'Defying US efforts, guerillas in Iraq refocus and strengthen', *New York Times*, 24 July 2005,

15 See David S. Cloud, 'Insurgents using bigger, more lethal bombs, US officers say', *New York Times*, 4 Aug. 2005.

16 Quoted from Dexter Filkin, 'Profusion of rebel groups helps them survive in Iraq', *New York Times*, 2 Dec. 2005.

17 Paul Virilio, 'Cold panic', *Cultural Politics*, 1 (2005), pp. 27–30.

18 See Elaine Sciolino, 'Europe meets the new face of terrorism', *New York Times*, 1 Aug. 2005.

19 See Larry Elliott, 'Rich spend 25 times more on defense than aid', *Guardian*, 6 July 2005.

20 Meacher, 'Playing Bin Laden's game'.

21 See Maurice Druon, 'Les stratégies aveugles', *Le Figaro*, 18 Nov. 2004, p. 13.

22 See Mark Juergensmeyer, 'Is religion the problem?', *Hedgehog Review*, Spring 2004, pp. 21–33.

23 Charles Kimball, *When Religion Becomes Evil*, Harper, 2002, p. 36.

24 See Henry A. Giroux, 'Rapture politics', *Toronto Star*, 24 July 2005.

25 See Martin Bright, 'Muslim leaders in feud with the BBC', *Observer*, 14 Aug. 2005.

26 Interview with Uri Avnery, *Tikkun*, Sept.–Oct. 2005, pp. 33–9.

27 Tzvetan Todorov, *Mémoire du mal, tentation du bien. Enquête sur le siècle*, Robert Laffont, 2000, pp. 139ff; Margarete Buber-Neumann, *La Révolution mondiale*, Casterman, 1971; and 'Mein Weg zum Kommunismus', in *Plädoyer für Freiheit und Menschlichkeit*, Hentrich, 2000.

28 See Jad Mouawad, 'Katrina's shock to the system', *New York Times*, 4 Sept. 2005.

29 See David Lyon, 'Technology vs. "terrorism": circuits of city surveillance since September 11, 2001', in *Cities, War and Terrorism: Towards an Urban Geopolitics*, ed. Stephen Graham, Blackwell, 2004, pp. 297–311.

30 Quoted after Sandra Lavikke, 'Victim of terror crackdown blames bombers for robbing him of freedom', *Guardian*, 4 Aug. 2005, p. 7.

31 See Ian Fisher, 'Italians say London suspect lacks wide terrorist ties', *New York Times*, 2 Aug. 2005.
32 Alan Trevis and Duncan Campbell, 'Bakir to be banned from UK', *Guardian*, 10 Aug. 2005.
33 See Benjamin R. Barber in conversation with Artur Domosławski, *Gazeta Wyborcza*, 24–6 Dec. 2004, pp. 19–20.

Chapter 5   Setting Fears Afloat

1 Robert Castel, *L'insécurité sociale. Qu'est-ce qu'être protégé?* Seuil, 2003, p. 5.
2 Ibid., p. 6.
3 David L. Altheide, 'Mass media, crime, and the discourse of fear', *Hedgehog Review*, 5, no. 3 (Fall 2003), pp. 9–25.
4 See Neal Lawson, *Dare More Democracy: From Steam-Age Politics to Democratic Self-Governance*, Compass, 2005.
5 Cf. Thomas Frank, *One Market under God*, Secker and Warburg, 2001.
6 Thomas Frank quoted in Lawson, *Dare More Democracy*.
7 See 'Awash in information, patients face a lonely, uncertain road', *New York Times*, 14 Aug. 2005.
8 See *The Complete Prose of Woody Allen*, Picador, 1980.
9 *Hedgehog Review*, 5, no. 3 (Fall 2003), pp. 5–7.
10 Caroline Roux, 'To die for', *Guardian Weekend*, 13 Aug. 2005.
11 Mary Douglas, *Natural Symbols: Explorations in Cosmology*, Pantheon Books, 1970, pp. 21ff.
12 Stephen Graham, 'Postmortem city: towards an urban geopolitics', *City*, 2 (2004), pp. 165–96.
13 Eduardo Mendietta, 'The axle of evil: SUVing through the slums of globalizing neoliberalism', *City*, 2 (2005), pp. 195–204.
14 Ray Surette, *Media, Crime and Criminal Justice*, Brooks/Cole, 1992, p. 43.
15 Loïc Wacquant, *Punir les pauvres. Le nouveau gouvernement de l'insécurité sociale*, Agone, 2004, pp. 11ff.
16 See Joseph Epstein, 'Celebrity culture', *Hedgehog Review* (Spring 2005), pp. 7–20.
17 Richard Rorty, 'Love and money', in Rorty, *Philosophy and Social Hope*, Penguin, 1999, p. 233.
18 John Dunn, *Setting the People Free*, Atlantic Books, 2005, p. 161.
19 Lawrence Grossberg, *Caught in a Crossfire*, Paradigm, 2005, p. 112.

20 Polly Toynbee, 'Free-market buccaneers', *Guardian*, 19 Aug. 2005. Gate Gourmet, a supranational company to which BA 'contracted out' its catering services, recently summarily fired its 670 employees after they took strike action against the hiring of cheaper labour offered by the temp agency Blue Arrow.

21 See Andy Beckett, 'The making of the terror myth', *Guardian*, 15 Oct. 2004, G2 pp. 2–3.

22 See Hugues Lagrange, *Demandes de sécurité*, Seuil, 2003.

23 See Deborah Orr, 'A relentless diet of false alarms and terror hype', *Independent*, 3 Feb. 2004, p. 33.

24 Richard Norton-Taylor, 'There's no such thing as total security', *Guardian*, 19 Aug. 2005.

25 See 'War on terror fuels small arms trade', *Guardian*, 10 Oct. 2003, p. 19.

26 See Conor Gearty, 'Cry Freedom', *Guardian*, G2, 3 Dec. 2004, p. 9.

27 See, in particular, the confidential file, nearly 2,000 pages long of the American Army criminal investigation, obtained by the *New York Times* and published on 28 May 2005.

28 See Neil A. Lewis, 'Interrogators cite doctors' aid at Guantanamo', *New York Times*, 24 June 2005.

29 See Eric Schmitt and Thom Shanker, 'New posts considered for US commanders after abuse', *New York Times*, 20 June 2005.

30 Beckett, 'The making of the terror myth'.

31 See Victor Grotowicz, *Terrorism in Western Europe: In the Name of the Nation and the Good Cause*, PWN (Warsaw), 2000.

32 Tzvetan Todorov, *Mémoire du mal, tentation du bien*, Robert Laffont, 2000, pp. 28–9.

33 See my *In Search of Politics*, Polity, 2000.

34 Quoted after Ken Hirschkop, 'Fear and democracy: an essay on Bakhtin's theory of carnival', *Associations*, 1 (1997), pp. 209–34.

35 Todorov, *Mémoire du mal*, p. 47.

36 Richard Rorty, *Achieving our Country*, Harvard University Press, 1998, pp. 83–4.

37 Ibid., p. 88.

38 Max Hastings, 'They've never had it so good', *Guardian*, 6 Aug. 2005.

Chapter 6   Thought against Fear

This chapter is an edited version of the Miliband Lecture delivered at the London School of Economics in November 2005.

1 See Jacques Derrida, *Chaque fois unique, la fin du monde*, presented by Pascale-Anne Brault and Michael Naas, Galilée, 2003.

2 See Alain Finkielkraut, *Nous autres, modernes*, Ellipses, 2005, p. 245.

3 See Adorno's letter to Benjamin of 18 March 1936, in Theodor Adorno and Walter Benjamin, *Correspondence, 1928–1940*, Harvard University Press, 1999, pp. 127–33.

4 Ibid., p. 14.

5 Theodor W. Adorno, *The Culture Industry: Selected Essays on Mass Culture*, ed. J. M. Bernstein, Routledge, 1991, p. 89.

6 Ibid., p. 119.

7 Ibid., p. 15.

8 Ibid., p. 128.

9 Ibid., pp. 292–3.

10 T. W. Adorno and M. Horkheimer, *Dialectic of Enlightenment*, Verso, 1989, p. 243.

11 T. W. Adorno, *Critical Models*, Columbia University Press, 1998, p. 263.

12 Ibid., p. 92.

13 Theodor W. Adorno, *Minima Moralia*, trans. E. F. N. Jephcott, Verso, 1974, p. 25.

14 Ibid., p. 26.

15 *La Misère du monde*, under the direction of Pierre Bourdieu, Seuil, 1993, pp. 1449–554. See also P. Bourdieu et al., *The Weight of the World*, Polity, 1999.

16 Claude Lanzmann and Robert Redeker, 'Les méfaits d'un rationalisme simplificateur', *Le Monde*, 18 Sept. 1998, p. 14.

17 See Jean-Pierre Dupuy, *Pour un catastrophisme éclairé. Quand impossible est certain*, Seuil, 2002, p. 167.

Index